An
Unexpected
Journey

An
Unexpected
Journey

Discovering Reformed Christianity

W. ROBERT GODFREY

P U B L I S H I N G
P.O. BOX 817 • PHILLIPSBURG • NEW JERSEY 08865-0817

Page design and typesetting by Lakeside Design Plus

Printed in the United States of America

Library of Congress Cataloging-in-Publication Data

Godfrey, W. Robert.
    An unexpected journey : discovering Reformed Christianity / W. Robert Godfrey.
        p. cm.
    ISBN 0-87552-719-1 (pbk.)
    1. Reformed Church. 2. Calvinism. I. Title.

BX9422.3.G64 2004
284'.2—dc22

                                                    2003067186

To my children,
William Charles Godfrey
Mari Anne Godfrey
Robert Manter Godfrey
who are making the journey with me.

Contents

Introduction

Calvinism has been one of the great forces in the history of Christianity. From the sixteenth century on, millions of Christians have found spiritual and intellectual fulfillment as well as the inspiration to live and suffer for Christ in the Reformed movement.

Today we continue to see the fruit of Calvinism in various denominations and theologies. But the appeal of historic Calvinism seems significantly diminished in our time. Many Christians have no knowledge about Calvinism as a great spiritual expression of the faith. The few who have are likely to know it only in relation to theology or scholarship. One example is the defense of the inerrancy of Scripture in the work of such men as B. B. Warfield, J. Gresham Machen, E. J. Young, J. I. Packer, R. C. Sproul, and James Montgomery Boice. The work of these Reformed scholars has often benefited evangelical Christians without their really understanding the faith that inspired it.

As important as the intellectual defense of the faith is, Christianity is more than theology. Much more. But how can we come to see and appreciate that comprehensive character of Calvinism?

One of the ways of seeing the vitality of a form of Christianity has been through the autobiographies of its adherents. Christian autobiography is an ancient and influential form of tracing the path of God's grace in one life. Augustine's *Confessions* (A.D. 401) is the most famous of this kind of early autobiography, recording his life and conversion. Augustine states his understanding of the purpose of relating personal experiences with God when he tells the story of the conversion of a Roman citizen named Victorinus. Augustine writes that he records Victorinus's experience because "the story glorifies Your grace and should be told to Your glory" (viii, 2).

In recent decades, several notable former evangelical Protestants have written autobiographical accounts of their conversions from Protestantism either to Roman Catholicism or to Eastern Orthodoxy. In doing so, they followed the nineteenth-century example of the Anglican John Henry Newman, who converted to Rome. These autobiographies have all tried to show the limits and frustrations of Protestantism and the attractions of pre-Reformation religion.

Reformed Christians through the centuries have written far fewer such autobiographies than have those in other traditions. We do have letters, journals, and diaries from Reformed writers, but not many of their own life stories. Reformed Christians have perhaps followed the attitude of John Calvin, who wrote in his famous *Reply to Sadoleto*, "I do not speak willingly about myself." Calvinists are better at theology than autobiography. They prefer talking about God rather than themselves.

The purpose of this book is not to try to reverse this Reformed reticence or simply to write an autobiography of my life. Rather, I hope that some reflection on my experience in coming to Reformed Christianity from the outside might clarify Calvinism's value and vitality on a personal level. For too many, Calvinism has seemed either an intellectual exercise in theology or an inherited and often unexamined religious commitment. But as I have experienced it, Reformed Christianity is not simply an inherited tradition or an expression of intellectual theology. I believe that Reformed Christianity is the best, fullest form of biblical religion. And with that provocative claim, I hope that you will read and reflect on what follows.

Special thanks again to Mary Ellen, my wife, who helped me envision this project, encouraged each step of the writing, edited chapters, and taught them to her Bible study class. Thanks to the Ladies Bible Study of the Escondido United Reformed Church for using this material and encouraging its publication. Thanks also to Allan Fisher and his fine staff at P&R for all of their labors on this book.

"A man's steps are directed by the LORD. How then can anyone understand his own way?" (Prov. 20:24)

Hearing About Calvinism—
God in Control

PSALM 139

As a junior in high school (1961–1962), I met my first Calvinist in a swimming pool. Paul Hoekenga and I were both on our high school swimming team in Alameda, California. Alameda was then a city of about 50,000, built on a flat island across the bay from San Francisco. Both Paul and I were from families with deep roots in Alameda. Several of my high school teachers had also taught my parents when they were students there.

Alameda High School was a large public school, and Paul was a year ahead of me—we would probably never have met except for the swimming team. It turned out that we lived rather close to each other at some distance from the school. So often after workout we had a long walk home together. We spoke of many things, from swimming to studies to politics.

Both of us were really better at studying than swimming. In time, our conversation turned to religion.

Paul was a member of the Christian Reformed Church in town. I knew nothing about that congregation or denomination. I was a Methodist, but I did not know much about that either. My grandparents and great-grandparents had been active in the Methodist Church, but my parents attended only very occasionally. I had been baptized, gone for several years to Sunday school, and been confirmed in the church, but I had learned very little. I do not remember the Bible's ever being opened in my home, but I know that I had been told (by my grandmother) and believed that the Bible was the Word of God.

My discussions about religion with Paul really piqued my interest; I realized how little I knew. In retrospect, I am amazed at how readily I accepted what I was hearing. It all seemed perfectly sensible and true. What I heard about God and Christ, about sin and grace, about judgment and redemption resonated with me.

Being a lover of books, I wanted to read about this Calvinism. I went to the public library to try to find out more. There I found a book by Ben Warburton, entitled *Calvinism*. It was not a comprehensive presentation of the Reformed faith, but rather a vigorous defense of what are often called the five points of Calvinism (total depravity, unconditional election, limited atonement, irresistible grace, and the perseverance of the saints). The book, I learned later, had been given to the library by the Christian Reformed Church.

Starting with the doctrine of sin and man's complete helplessness to find salvation, the book showed from the Bible and by good theological reflection that God and God alone was the author of the plan of salvation. Christ fulfilled that plan by his righteous life and atoning death, and the Holy Spirit applied the work of Christ to sinners, who could in no way help themselves. This message seemed obviously right to me. The book began with total depravity, and from that beginning it was clear that all of salvation must come from God—the God who had planned that salvation from all eternity.

Because I loved to read, I later borrowed from the pastor of the Christian Reformed Church, the Rev. Harold Petroelje, a copy of John Calvin's *Institutes of the Christian Religion*. He told me years later that he had not had many requests for that book from high school students. I cannot really remember now how much of it I read at the time. But that early acquaintance with Calvin has grown and deepened over the years, and I continue to believe that Calvin was the most balanced and biblical theologian that the church has ever seen.

Looking back on that time, I believe that one particular part of Calvinism's message appealed to me. It was the teaching of a great and sovereign God who was truly in charge of all things. That teaching connected with thoughts and feelings that I had had while still quite young. For a time, years before I was a junior, as I lay in bed at night I would sense a great pointlessness to life, a great emptiness in the center of my being. The reality of death seemed to render all of life gray and hopeless—at least at moments when I lay in bed about to go to sleep. *What meaning could life have?* I wondered. Those sentiments may seem strange in a youngster, and they probably are unusual, especially for one raised in a happy family and pleasant circumstances. I suppose that I am expressing them now in words that I could not have found then. But the feelings themselves were real and intense.

Only years later would I come to a theological explanation for those early feelings. Ecclesiastes tells us, "He has also set eternity in the hearts of men" (3:11). Perhaps with that verse

15

in his mind Augustine wrote, right at the beginning of his *Confessions,* "You have made us for yourself and our hearts are restless until they rest in you." Because human beings are creatures, they cannot feel complete or whole except in a proper relationship with their Creator. Separated from their Creator, their restlessness can take many forms, and they can seek rest in many false sources. For me, a fear of death and meaninglessness had been my restlessness. By the grace of the Holy Spirit, the message of Calvinism would in time give me rest.

I was drawn to the God of the Bible, the God presented in Calvinism, because of his essential nature and character. I began to learn that the true God is self-sufficient. He does not need me. That humbling thought is critical if humans are to achieve a proper vision of their own worth. God is not dependent on us, but we are dependent on him. And that self-sufficient God is unchanging. He is so complete and full in himself that he does not need to improve or develop. From everlasting to everlasting, he is God. He is not determined by outside influences. He does not age or decay.

Psalm 102 declares of the heavens and the earth in relation to God: "They will perish, but you remain" (v. 26). The most apparently stable elements of creation will change and fade, but God remains the same. What a remarkable thought! At the center of all the whirl that we experience, God is steady and stable and completely reliable. When we remember with the psalmist, "For my days vanish like smoke; my bones burn like glowing embers," we need not despair (v. 3). God continues as the immovable foundation of our lives.

David elaborates on the character of God in Psalm 139. He celebrates a God who knows everything about me (vv. 1–6). (And by implication, if he knows everything about one little person, then he knows everything about everything.) He knows where I am and what I am doing. He knows what I am think-ing and the words that I will speak even before I know them. I am surrounded by him and by his knowledge of me as the mountains surround Jerusalem and as the angel of the Lord surrounded the camp of Israel in the wilderness (Ps. 125:2; Ps. 34:7). He knows me completely.

God is also always present with me (Ps. 139:7–12). Whether I go to the highest heavens or the deepest sea or travel to a distant point on the earth, God is as fully present there as anywhere else. Even the most profound darkness cannot hide me from God for he is there as well, present with me and know-ing me completely. Whether I was in the swimming pool, the classroom, or the bedroom at night, God was there.

The God who knows me and is with me is the God who created me. From my first beginning in the womb, it was God who gave me life and formed my growth and development. Here we see the personal character of the God of the Bible. God is not an impersonal force. Nor is he a splendid being so exalted and remote as to be indifferent and removed from the lives of individual humans. Rather, he is personally related to us and involved with us from the first moment of our existence.

We also see his amazing power. He formed me as a new creature coming into being just as he originally formed every-thing else that was created. As he forms the baby in the womb, so he formed the universe and everything in it in the begin-ning. The personal care of God in no way reduces the grandeur of his power displayed in all of creation. "Your works are won-derful, I know that full well" (Ps. 139:14).

Finally, we should notice that the Bible knows no sepa-ration between what we call the processes of nature and the personal work of God. The growth of a baby in the womb is natural, but it is at the same time at each moment the very activity of God. God usually uses natural means to accomplish his purposes, but those means are never separate from his personal care and action.

God, the personal and powerful Creator, acts according to his eternal plan: "All the days ordained for me were written in your book before one of them came to be" (v. 16). He governs the world absolutely according to the wisdom of his eternal plan. God is not a quarterback, ducking and weaving and improvising in the face of the enemy. God always knows the end from the beginning and accomplishes all things according to his will. And that will is absolutely wise and profound—often beyond our ability to comprehend. "Such knowledge is too wonderful for me, too lofty for me to attain" (v. 6). As the apostle Paul said, "Oh, the depth of the riches of the wisdom and knowledge of God! How unsearchable his judgments, and his paths beyond tracing out!" (Rom. 11:33).

In my early days as a Calvinist, I thought more about God's power in history than about his power in creation. I had always been very interested in history. From my earliest days of reading, I had enjoyed learning about other times and places and people. I liked the heroism of the stories, but I also appreciated that the historical accounts implied an order and meaning and purpose in history. As I learned to know God, I especially appreciated that he was the one who was behind all the movement in history. He ensured that history would fulfill his purpose and that it therefore had meaning—even if I could not see it.

We call the way in which God governs history and all things by his great plan the doctrine of providence. For Calvinists, it is a foundational expression of the greatness of God. One of the fine Reformed statements of faith, the Heidelberg Catechism, defines providence as "the almighty and everywhere present power of God, whereby, as it were by his hand, he still upholds heaven and earth, with all creatures, and so governs them that herbs and grass, rain and drought, fruitful and barren years, meat and drink, health and sickness, riches and poverty, yea, all things, come not by chance, but by his fatherly hand" (Q and A 27). The catechism, to which I was first introduced at the Alameda CRC, reminds us that such a truth is important and profitable for us so that "we may be patient in adversity, thankful in prosperity, and for what is future have good confidence in our faithful God and Father that no creature shall separate us from his love, since all creatures are so in his hand that without his will they cannot so much as move" (Q and A 28).

This powerful and personal God of providence is also a God of justice and mercy (Ps. 139:19–24). In strong terms, the psalmist identifies with the justice of God that will judge the wicked. He also rejoices in the mercy of God that will forgive him and lead him in the way everlasting. The universe that God has created and now governs is at its deepest level a moral universe because God is a moral being. This great God about whom Calvinists taught me was the God I found in the Bible and the God who met the restlessness of my heart.

I know that for some people, the idea of a God who is so fully in charge raises serious questions. If God is sovereign, how do we explain evil? If God is sovereign, how can I be responsible? Am I just a robot in his plan? If God is unchanging and all-powerful, can he be personal and caring? These are important questions that deserve careful answers. I can only say at this point that as I began to embrace Calvinism, they were not questions that really troubled me. I felt responsible and knew that God said I was responsible. That was enough for me. I also experienced the care of God in the Christian community that I came to know in the Alameda Christian Reformed Church. In time I would come to understand much more clearly than I did in the beginning that the mercy and care of God is seen fully only in Jesus.

The beginning of my pilgrimage to Calvinism began with thinking about God. It amazes me how many people do not really think about God. Some just ignore him and resist all efforts to discuss him. They seem able to face life and death without dealing with probing questions: Where did I come from? Who or what gives meaning and moral direction to life? What happens after I die? Others seem to think of God only in relation to some problem of their own that they hope he will solve. Often they create a god that pleases them—usually a god created in their own image. They seem to want a god that will serve them rather than the true God whom they should serve.

In American culture today, many people seem to feel a special need for affirmation and attention. Some have called this a therapeutic culture in which we are looking for a remedy for our problems. In this culture, we see efforts to turn God into the great therapist. We are told that he feels our pain and understands our struggles because he struggles too. He too is surprised and hurt by the course of history and of our lives. But he cares so much that he finds ways of solving our problems, at least until the next surprising problem comes along.

This new view of God as one who feels, suffers, and changes claims to be biblical. But in fact, this view rejects the Christian God as understood in all ages of the church by Roman Catholics, Eastern Orthodox, and Protestants. More importantly, this view flies in the face of what the Bible says over and over again about God as the one who does not change and who knows the end from the beginning. This new god is more like the Zeus of ancient paganism than the God of the

Bible. We must beware of these convenient gods that we invent for ourselves and believe only in the God revealed in the Bible.

In light of my fearfulness about change as a child, I need to ask: did I simply create a God in my mind to meet my needs? I do not think so. For years I have compared my understanding of God with what I find in the Bible. And I find in the Bible a revelation of precisely that God about whom the Calvinists taught me in the beginning. This God does indeed meet the real needs of my heart. That is because he made me, and my heart was restless until it rested in him. I had within me what Calvin called a sense of divinity; by God's grace, that sense grew not into idolatry, but into a love for what the Bible says about God.

Experiencing a Congregation

PSALM 84

My friend Paul invited me to attend church with him, and one Sunday morning I entered my first Reformed church. I had occasionally been to the Methodist church, of which my family were members, so some aspects of a worship service were not unfamiliar to me. But I can still vividly recall certain striking aspects of that first Reformed service. First, I noticed that the church was rather full and that the congregation consisted of families and people of all ages. When I occasionally attended our Methodist church (a large building) with my grandmother, there always seemed to be rather few worshipers—most of them older women. I can remember attending a Good Friday service there and thinking in my teenage mind as I looked around, "All these people are so old that next year I might be the only one here." By contrast, to see in the Christian Reformed Church children and men in significant numbers and to see families sitting together was remarkable for me.

My second impression was of the singing. It was vigorous and loud. My memory of singing in our Methodist church was that I never heard anything other than my own voice and the organ. But the Reformed people seemed to know the songs well, and they sang them in a heartfelt way. I did not know those songs, but I found the singing of the congregation very encouraging.

My third impression was that the service was as simple as the architecture of the church. Our Methodist church had stained-glass windows with biblical scenes, an altar, candles, and crosses—all of which were absent from the Reformed church. As the church building did not make use of decorative symbols, so the service lacked ritual or ceremony beyond the elements of worship. The minister, dressed in ordinary clothes, led us in Bible readings, prayers, and singing that were straightforward and clear.

My last memory of those earliest visits was the seriousness of the worship. Most everyone was seated in church and observed a reverent quiet before the service began. There was no chattering or conversation. Then the minister, together with the elders and the deacons, entered the church (after praying together before the service, as I learned later). The pastoral prayer was serious in its language and length and varied in its content, lasting 10 to 15 minutes. It was difficult for me to pay attention to the prayer as carefully as I knew I should, but I was still impressed that speaking to God was such an important part of the service. The sermon as an explanation and application of the Bible also demonstrated a carefulness about worship, and I sensed that we were being called into the presence of God.

As the months passed, I became more and more attracted to the deep sense of community that I experienced in that congregation. I discovered that natural affinities contributed to this community. Several families were related to one another, and most were ethnically Dutch. A number were from the Midwest and had attended the same schools. But beyond those factors was a strong common commitment of faith and a real love and caring for one another.

That sense of community expressed a critical part of biblical religion. From the beginning of creation, God had revealed that it was not good for man to be alone. Human beings are fulfilled in families and communities. Throughout the Bible God deals as much with families, tribes, nations, and congregations as he docs with individuals. The Bible often compares the church to a family. In my first Reformed church, I saw that ideal of community given concrete expression in the love and care of the people for me.

I am sure that in a number of ways I was a surprise to those in the congregation who came to know me. This was not a church accustomed to many visitors from the community. Some knew of my father's involvement in city politics. He would later become mayor. Some even knew of my grandfather's work to reform city government before the Second World War, which led to a city park being named after him. I know that the intellectual curiosity that I showed about Calvinism was not typical of most juniors in high school. But people were amazingly patient and helpful. I enjoyed the hospitality of both young people my age and adults.

Again and again I was invited to meals and never sensed restlessness when I stayed too long to ask my questions. Especially Paul and Gertrude Hoekenga and Jack and Bernie Andriese gave very generously of themselves in those high school years. I also profited from Sunday school classes and Young People's Society where we studied and discussed the Scriptures and the faith. I particularly remember the studies in the book of Romans led with such care by Harold Camping for the Young People. In those days, Camping had not yet developed his peculiar views of Bible teaching,[1] but simply presented a traditional Reformed interpretation of Romans—taking seven years to work through the book. These people gave to me a great deal of their time out of love for me and for Christ. They enfolded me into their community.

The church is both an institution and a body linked by faith and love. Too often these two dimensions of the church have been set against one another. In the Roman Catholic Church, for example, so much attention is given to precise institutional form and function that little effort is made to create real community among people. Among some charismatic churches, by contrast, little attention is given to institutional forms or disciplines, but great effort is made to create a community of common experience. Yet churches that follow the Bible should care about both. Scripture clearly lays down directions for officers, forms of worship, and varieties of discipline for the church as an institution. But it also directs that the church members know and care for one another, not only when they gather as a whole community, but in other contexts as well. When a congregation has both a biblical form and loving connections among the members, true Christian community becomes a light shining in a dark world.

Psalm 84 expresses in poetic form much of what I experienced of the church in those early days. The psalmist writes of the temple in Jerusalem as the focus of his feelings about the community of God with his people. For New Testament Christians, those feelings are ours as we remember that Hebrews 12

1. Sadly, Harold Camping later developed a spiritualizing interpretation of the Bible that has led him to the heretical conclusion that believers ought to leave their churches because the era of the church is over.

shows us that the church—especially at worship—communes with God in the heavenly temple in the heavenly Jerusalem.

First, the psalmist celebrates the attractiveness of the temple. "How lovely is your dwelling place, O LORD Almighty! My soul yearns, even faints, for the courts of the LORD; my heart and my flesh cry out for the living God" (Ps. 84:1–2). Here the theme of beauty is not a matter of architecture, but of being in the presence of God. God's people long for him as he comes to them in the institutions that he has established. The courts and sacrifices of the temple are now fulfilled in Christ, but by his Spirit he is even more present with us in Scripture, sermon, and sacrament. As Paul wrote to the Colossians, "Therefore do not let anyone judge you by what you eat or drink, or with regard to a religious festival, a New Moon celebration or a Sabbath day. These are a shadow of the things that were to come; the reality, however, is found in Christ" (2:16–17). Here we see the Mosaic institutions passing away. Of the spiritual life in the New Covenant, Paul wrote, "Let the word of Christ dwell in you richly as you teach and admonish one another with all wisdom, and as you sing psalms, hymns and spiritual songs with gratitude in your hearts to God" (Col. 3:16).

As we understand how truly present God is with us in worship, we long even more for that fellowship with God. The church is truly home for us. We are drawn to God and his worship as a bird is drawn to its nest. Psalm 42:1–2 expresses that eager desire: "As the deer pants for streams of water, so my soul pants for you, O God. My soul thirsts for God, for the living God. When can I go and meet with God?"

Second, worship is a communal experience. We do not worship alone but with fellow believers: "Blessed are *those* who dwell in your house; *they* are ever praising you" (Ps. 84:4). Other psalms stress this point. "These things I remember as I pour out my soul:

how I used to go with the multitude, leading the procession to the house of God, with shouts of joy and thanksgiving among the festive throng" (Ps. 42:4). Psalm 55:14 is even clearer as it remembers a friend "with whom I once enjoyed sweet fellowship as we walked with the throng at the house of God."

The joy of the church's worship is not the solitary relationship of one soul with God. Rather, it is the joy and sweetness of joining with others who share a common faith and desire. The community of believers both encourages and multiplies the experience of worship. Perhaps that is why so many psalms not only address God, but also call on fellow worshipers to join in praising him. We see this communal theme also in Hebrews. First, we are admonished, "And let us consider how we may spur one another on toward love and good deeds. Let us not give up meeting together, as some are in the habit of doing, but let us encourage one another—and all the more as you see the Day approaching" (Heb. 10:24–25).

Second, we are encouraged by the vision of the heavenly company that we already keep: "But you have come to Mount Zion, to the heavenly Jerusalem, the city of the living God. You have come to thousands upon thousands of angels in joyful assembly, to the church of the firstborn, whose names are written in heaven. You have come to God, the judge of all men, to the spirits of righteous men made perfect, to Jesus the mediator of a new covenant, and to the sprinkled blood that speaks a better word than the blood of Abel" (Heb. 12:22–24).

Third, Reformed worship is strong and a key source of strength for the believer. "Blessed are those whose strength is in you, who have set their hearts on pilgrimage. . . . They go from strength to strength, till each appears before God in Zion" (Ps. 84:5, 7). Such worship is not sentimental or cloying; it is not trivial or superficial. Rather, it is demanding of attention, reflection, involvement, and commitment. The depth and riches in readings, songs, and teaching are the material from which a maturing Christian life is built.

The church as such a community is especially needed in our day. Community is threatened in many ways in our modern world. Most of us do not live in traditional neighborhoods. Oh, we have neighbors, but at most we have only a nodding acquaintance with almost all of them. No real sense of community exists in many apartment buildings, condos, and suburban streets. The result is often a sense of isolation and alienation. Our families too, as communities, today are at risk. So many marriages end in divorce that community is often broken between parents and for children. Even in families that are not broken by divorce, the busyness of life is a grave problem. Whether at work, on the road, at school or at lessons for children outside of school, or even at church, families often have little time together, except perhaps to watch TV.

The temptation then is to create substitutes that feel a little like community but are really entirely different. For some, TV or pets take the place of true human communities. Others seek community as spectators at sporting events that consume an amazing amount of time, money, and conversation. Still others seek a community of alcohol in a bar. But none of these associations are real communities of love and concern.

Even churches too often become only apparent communities. In many places today, worship has become a spectacle or entertainment whose focus is more on human performance than on God. The response to such worship is not so much faith and repentance, but amazement, appreciation, and applause. Many contemporary churches have become like ancient Greek theaters where the aim of the gathering was catharsis—a heightening of emotions with a healing effect.

Those at such churches may leave feeling happier, but are they in reality closer to God and growing in grace?

Other churches may be bound together only by ethnicity or tradition. The habit of gathering may drive them, or a purely human concern may guide them. They may even have real human community. But are they a community of Christ's church? The danger is that the God revealed in Scripture is not the source and center of their life together.

Still other churches may exist really only as debating societies. This danger besets some Reformed churches. They behave as if they primarily exist as a gathering of theologians to feud about particular points of doctrine. Although doctrinal precision and theology are critical to the church, they are not its only concern, nor are they the calling and responsibility of all members equally.

All these aberrant forms of Christian community, whether of experience, emotion, tradition, or debate, fail to be what Christ founded the church to be. The church must be a community of commitment and loving concern for the lives of others.

The church today needs to be a community of people in communion with God and one another. Why? First, that is what God has called the church to be. And second, such a church community can be the most effective Christian witness to our community-starved land. As we have learned from the Heidelberg Catechism (86), we do good works in part so that "by our godly living our neighbors may be won over to Christ." That truth and experience I learned in my first Reformed church. Although I was shy and different in background and interests, Reformed Christians took time to answer my questions and to be my friends. For them I was not just a soul to save, but a person to love and help grow in Christ and in his church.

THREE

Getting Acquainted
with the Bible

PSALM   119:97-144

When I began regularly attending church as a junior in high
school, I soon discovered how very central the Bible was in the
life of the church. I also discovered that I knew very little about
the Bible—which can be an intimidating book for a newcomer.
Christians become so familiar with the Bible that they take
some knowledge of it for granted. But I have heard comments
such as these made by unchurched people: "The New Testament is a better translation than the Old Testament"; "I am
never going back to that Bible study because the leader asked
everyone to turn to Mark, and I was the only one who didn't
know what that meant." As far as I can remember, however,
my ignorance of the Bible was not a problem for me. I was
curious about what the Bible said. People in the congregation
helped me learn, and I do not recall any discomfort in my early

days among those who knew much about the Bible when I knew nothing.

The centrality of the Bible was evident to me in many ways. First, its importance was visually prominent in the church. A large Bible was visible on the pulpit in the front of the church. In the pew racks next to the hymnals were Bibles for worshipers to use in church. A number of people carried their own Bibles to church. A variety of translations were present among the people, including the King James Version, the Revised Standard Version, and the Berkeley translation. But the pew Bibles were the American Standard Version always read in public worship. This translation was valued, I was told, because it was a literal rendering of the biblical text (and was affectionately known as the "Jehovah Version" because the divine name in the Old Testament was translated as *Jehovah*).

Even more impressive than the visible presence of the Bible was the extensive use that was made of it in church. The sermons in public worship were careful expositions and applications of the Scriptures. A substantial portion of the Bible was read in the service as a distinct and important act of worship. We experienced firsthand the instruction that Paul had given to Timothy to "devote yourself to the public reading of Scripture, to preaching and to teaching" (1 Tim. 4:13). In Sunday school class and Young People's Society, the study of the Bible was the central activity.

The attitude in approaching the Bible was the same in all these contexts. First, the Bible was approached reverently. Even when I knew little about the Bible, I sensed that dealing with it was a serious and sacred matter. I remember one discussion in Young People's about whether we really ought to kneel when we read the Bible privately out of reverence for God's Word. We always began our study of the Bible with prayer that the

Lord would bless us in our study. The words "Let us open in prayer" became so familiar to me that when I was a freshman at Stanford University and my German professor began the first class with the words, "Let us open . . .," I had started to fold my hands and close my eyes before he said, ". . . to the first page of our grammar."

Second, the Bible was read confidently. The whole of Scripture was treated as the Word of God. Our attitude was not that of those who stand over the Bible in judgment as to its truthfulness or as those who try to distinguish the Word of God from the word of men in the Bible. We believed that the whole Bible was true and completely reliable. We also came to the Bible expectantly. We knew that the Bible was profitable for God's people. We expected that as we studied, we would grow in grace and understanding of God's purpose for our lives.

The attitudes that I found in the church toward the Bible were the same as those that the psalmist expressed in his great celebration of the Word of God in Psalm 119. In that psalm we first see his profound sense of the trustworthiness of the Word. In almost every verse, the psalmist acknowledges that the Word is "your" Word; this is God's Word. Although God used human authors, the Word is in every sense God's own declaration. The Word evokes awe: "Your statutes are wonderful . . ." (v. 129). It is also entirely reliable: "The statutes you have laid down are righteous; they are fully trustworthy" (v. 138); "Your righteousness is everlasting and your law is true" (v. 142); "Your statutes are forever right" (v. 144). No shadow of untruth is found in the Bible.

The Word also gives clear directions to the believer for faith and life. Understanding comes from the Bible: "Your commands make me wiser than my enemies, for they are ever with me. I have more insight than all my teachers, for I meditate on your statutes. I have more understanding than the elders, for I obey your precepts" (Ps. 119:98–100). Wisdom for living before the Lord comes from his Word. No traditions of men or mystical experiences are necessary to supplement that Word. It is full and complete in itself. Those who rely on the Word are wiser than teachers or elders who fail to do so. That Word illumines dark places: "Your word is a lamp to my feet and a light for my path" (v. 105). It helps the believer avoid every wicked choice in the Christian life: "I gain understanding from your precepts; therefore I hate every wrong path" (v. 104); "Direct my footsteps according to your word; let no sin rule over me" (v. 133).

The biblical attitude toward the Bible, which I found in my Reformed church, related not only to the character of the Bible but also to its content. At the church I learned not just the stories of the Bible, but the system of truth and life revealed in the Bible. Let me explain what I mean.

In many churches and Sunday school classes, well-meaning preachers and teachers have presented the Bible simply as a collection of stories. Now, of course, in one sense much of the Bible *is* a series of stories. From Adam to Noah, from Abraham to Joseph, from Moses to David, from Jesus to Paul, the Bible is rich in fascinating glimpses of the lives and activities of important and interesting people. Such stories are attractive to children and also to adults. Learning and telling those stories is a useful way of acquiring a knowledge of the Bible's content.

Such an approach, however, has serious limitations. One limitation is that many parts of the Bible are left out. Large sections of the Scriptures are not stories. Stories are a good approach to the historical sections of the Bible, but they do not work for the laws of the Pentateuch or the poetry of the

Psalms and Proverbs or the visions of the prophets or the instruction of the epistles. Treating the Bible as stories means that we know only part of the Bible and its meaning.

Yet a still more serious problem faces us in seeing the Bible as stories. This second limitation results from the uses made of the stories in the Bible. We can identify many evangelicals' use of the stories by the title of the children's hymn "Dare to Be a Daniel." In this way of presenting the stories, they are treated not just as interesting and inspiring bits of history. They are turned into moral examples of the way that we are to live. Teachers eagerly tell the story of Daniel—how as a young man in the court of the king of Babylon he abstained from eating foods forbidden by the law and refused to worship false idols. After telling this heroic tale, many teachers then say to their classes, "So you too should be faithful and courageous. You too should live for God without compromise with this world. Dare to be a Daniel!"

Such advice is in some ways good and useful, but is it what God means the story of Daniel to teach us? The story of Daniel is really a part of the great story of the ways in which God preserves a people for his name. The book of Daniel shows us how God protects his own even when he is punishing them in the exile. The Lord delivers his people from many dangers at the hands of their enemies in order to bring forth from them his Christ, the one who will save his people from their sins.

The motive of many evangelicals in using the Bible as stories teaching moral precepts was laudable. They wanted to inspire God's people to holy living through moral examples and imperatives. But this approach prepared the way for what we see in many churches today. If the recurring message found in the Scriptures is a word of moral exhortation, then it is in fact a small step from "dare to be a Daniel" to "don't get burned out the way Elijah did" or "learn five ways to manage your money from Solomon." A number of churches have moved from stories as moral examples to stories as psychological therapy. Theology is lost to therapy.

"How to Deal with Your Stress." "How to Manage Your Money." "How to Raise Your Children." These titles are not courses offered at your local community college. They are titles of sermons appearing rather often on the signboards and in the advertisements of churches. And these churches are not liberal churches, but rather evangelical congregations that would insist on their belief in the Bible.

Concern about stress, money, and children is understandable in a society that is falling apart. Those using the Bible to preach such themes believe that they are making Christianity relevant to the needs of our time. They believe that they are making the faith seem attractive and practical to the unchurched. In other words, they want to try to save our culture, our families, and our souls. But the irony is that the evangelicals—whose very name derives from *evangel*, "the gospel"—are in danger of losing the gospel in the process. They are allowing the felt needs of the unchurched to shape the message of the church. Sociology and psychology replace the Bible as the real authority in the life of the church. The study of the Bible, then, yields only sociological and psychological insights.

Such uses of the Scriptures may be understandable in the context of our world. But they miss the real meaning of the Word of God. They also miss the real need of the unchurched—namely, the gospel of the grace of Jesus Christ. To find that real meaning, we must turn from stories to a system.

No doubt many who hear the word "system" with reference to the Bible recoil. They have learned to regard the Bible and system as mutually exclusive. They believe that the Bible is a wonderful, moving book of stories, whereas a system is cold and rationalistic. Worst of all, they see a system as something that men (particularly Calvinists!) impose on the Bible. But the idea of the Bible as systematic truth is not cold, deadening, or forced. Rather, that idea is inherent in the teaching of the Bible about God and about itself. The God of the Bible is truth, and that truth is coherent in him. He is not a mass of irrational or internally contradictory truths. He is always consistent with himself. And since the Bible is the revelation of that God, the Bible too is internally consistent. It is not bits and pieces of religious thoughts that bear no relation to one another. The Bible is rather a progressive unfolding of God's plan and activity to save his people in Jesus Christ. The Bible moves from God's creating mankind for fellowship with him, to the breaking of that fellowship through sin, to God's work to gather a people out of fallen mankind and from that people to bring a Savior into the world. Here is the great message of the Bible, and everything in Scripture contributes to making that message clear.

The Bible is a book from which a clear and coherent system of doctrine emerges. For many today, the word *doctrine* is even worse than the word *system*. But *doctrine* is simply an English form of the Latin word *doctrina,* "teaching." To say that the Bible contains doctrine is to say that the Bible contains teaching. Reformed Christians have always believed that the teachings of the Bible form a system that can be comprehended, expressed, and summarized. That summary is expressed in the confessions of our churches.

The great system of the Bible, briefly stated, is that God created man good, but man rebelled against God, lost his original goodness, and lost any ability to restore his relationship with God. To redeem fallen man, God formed a people from whom his own eternal Son would be born as a man. That Son, Jesus, perfectly obeyed that law of God, suffered on the cross bearing the wrath of God in the place of his people, rose gloriously from the dead, and ever lives to rule over and protect his people. One day Jesus will return in glory to make all things new. In the meantime, his church is to preach his gospel, calling sinners to faith in him and to new life in him. The great message of the Bible from beginning to end is that God was in Christ reconciling the world to himself (2 Cor. 5:19).

As the church teaches this great system of the Bible, it will focus on God, on Christ, on sin, and on the grace of salvation. Although it may be useful to overcome stress and raise good children, that is not the primary message of the Bible or the primary duty of the church. Christ calls his church to make the great things of the Bible plain in a fallen world. Otherwise, the church loses the Bible—and the gospel.

In the early months of my first acquaintance with the Bible, I had an experience that helped me even in those early days to move beyond the story of the Bible to seeing its meaning in the system of biblical truth. I was in a Bible study at church looking at Mark's gospel. One day we were studying Mark 6:30–44, Jesus' feeding of the five thousand. We would probably have concluded that as a story, this passage teaches us to care for the physical well-being of Jesus' disciples. (And of course, we should have such concerns.) But we paused to ask in relation to verse 43 why twelve baskets of food were left over after the crowd had been fed. We might have concluded from this story that we ought to be generous, giving more than was needed. But as we looked more carefully, I saw that in Mark 6:7 Jesus had called the Twelve to him and then sent them out to minister in his name. We read that they did much effective work (v. 13) and then returned with no time to eat (v. 31). Jesus planned to take them aside to refresh them, but a crowd gathered and Jesus as the good shepherd had compassion on those in the crowd and taught them (v. 34). When everyone became hungry, the disciples wanted to send the crowd away (vv. 35–36). When the disciples thought they could not feed everyone (v. 37), Jesus fed them miraculously by multiplying five loaves and two fish (v. 41). Through the twelve baskets, Jesus showed the Twelve that he would commission them as his undershepherds and equip them with all that they would need in his service. Here was much more than just a story about sharing. Here was the founding commission for the apostles to be shepherds to Christ's flock. Here was a revelation of the character of the church. I began to see something of the depths and interconnectedness of the Bible's message.

The confidence that I learned to have in the Bible's character and content is rejected in a variety of ways in our time. The church helped me to be ready to face attacks on the Bible. And the people of God have faced such attacks in every generation. The psalmist long ago wrote, "The wicked have set a snare for me, but I have not strayed from your precepts" (Ps. 119:110).

Today that attack on the full trustworthiness of the Bible comes in many forms. Some see the Bible as simply a record of human religious experience from which one may or may not learn something useful. Others believe that the Bible contains the Word of God in the midst of other human thoughts that are not true. Still others believe that the Bible is the Word of God, although flawed with a few errors. All of these approaches to the Bible require that we as students become the judges of Scripture, separating truth from error. But God has revealed his Word to be the judge of our thinking and living. His Word is completely true and shows us the errors in our lives. For sinners to stand in judgment of the trustworthiness of any part of the Scriptures is to let the prisoners run the prison.

In response to these various attacks on the Scriptures, Bible-believing Christians (Reformed and non-Reformed) have come to refer to the Bible as inerrant—that is, without error. That doctrine of inerrancy I first learned in the Christian Reformed Church. I learned that the Bible was inspired by God, breathed out by him (2 Tim. 3:16), so it is as free from error as God himself is.

Because the Bible is inerrant, the very Word of God, we know that, far from deceiving us, the Bible will protect us. "You are my refuge and my shield; I have put my hope in your word" (Ps. 119:114). And "Sustain me according to your promise, and I will live; do not let my hopes be dashed" (v. 116).

Because the Scriptures are true and so useful and because they are the gift of our God to us, laying out his plan of salvation, we come to love and treasure them. The study of the Bible is not a burden, but a blessing eagerly anticipated by the people of God. The psalmist wrote, "Oh, how I love your law! I meditate on it all day long" (Ps. 119:97). And "How sweet are your promises to my taste, sweeter than honey to my mouth!" (v. 103). If we are God's people, we find joy in the Word: "Your statutes are my heritage forever; they are the joy of my heart" (v. 111). In the fellowship of that Reformed church in Alameda, I came to love and reverence the Bible as God's own Word.

Disciplines for Christian Living

One warm summer Sunday I was sitting in my new church listening to the sermon. From the middle of the church a young father rose and took his young son outdoors for misbehavior. He spanked the child—without realizing that he was doing so under the open windows of the church. As the boy cried, many in church could not help smiling. Soon the father returned to church with his son for the rest of the service. The son seemed to have learned something because he sat quietly through the rest of the service. I learned something too. This was a church in which there was seriousness of purpose and discipline.

In fact, a variety of disciplines surrounded me in this Reformed community. Most members attended church morning and evening every Sunday. They brought their children with them, teaching the children from a very young age to sit quietly. (My friend Paul reported that his father dealt subtly with unrest by twisting the skin on the forearm.) But discipline showed itself in much more than church attendance and punishment for misbehavior. The members dedicated their time and resources to Christian living.

Many in the congregation participated in studies of one sort or another. Bible studies, Sunday school classes, and catechism classes encouraged believers to be growing in a knowledge of the things of God. Young people (the preferred title of high school students like me) had Sunday school before the morning service and Young People's Society meeting after the evening service. After school one day during the week they had catechism class—a study of the Heidelberg Catechism—taught by the pastor. I always wondered why no one ever invited me to the catechism class. My educated guess today is that none of my high school friends could imagine that anyone would willingly go to catechism.

Many in the congregation were involved in a wide variety of Christian activities outside the church. Some worked to maintain Alameda's Christian elementary school, which members of the congregation had founded and continued to support with their gifts and their children. Others worked in organizations such as the Gideons, Christian radio, and Bible Study Fellowship.

Their discipline showed in the practices of piety pursued at home. Personal disciplines of Bible reading, meditation, and prayer were encouraged and widely practiced. Each meal began and ended with prayer. Usually the Bible was read while the family was still at the table after dinner. In some homes the Bible was read after every meal. I found this practice fascinating, but those raised with it were not always so excited. I remember after a meal listening to such a Bible reading. Suddenly the mother interrupted the father, pointed to one of the children, and said, "Last word." I froze, having no idea what this was about. I soon realized that it was a test to see whether the child was paying attention and could repeat the last word read from the Bible.

These various disciplines—aspects of which seem strange or amusing today—were not all unique to the Reformed tradition. But for the Reformed they followed from a passion to work out the implications of the Bible, particularly a verse such as Ephesians 5:15: "Be very careful, then, how you live—not as unwise but as wise. . . ." They lived out the conviction that the Christian life must be lived with care and thoughtfulness. Paul calls us to "find out what pleases the Lord" (Eph. 5:10) and to "understand what the Lord's will is" (Eph. 5:17).

The disciplines of careful living that I observed in the congregation can perhaps be divided into three areas: disciplines of the mind, disciplines of action, and disciplines of time. These disciplines overlap in a variety of ways, but by distinguishing them in this way we can see different ways in which the Reformed Christian seeks to live carefully.

The disciplines of the mind reflect the conviction that left to ourselves we live "as the Gentiles do, in the futility of their thinking. They are darkened in their understanding and separated from the life of God because of the ignorance that is in them due to the hardening of their hearts" (Eph. 4:17–18). This language is strong and offensive to many today: hard hearts, ignorance, and darkened understanding. We live in a world where we constantly hear that people are good, that they must look for the truth within themselves, that they should follow their instincts and intuition. Calvinists, by contrast, believe that we need the revelation of God precisely because we are so prone to be unwise. We are not just neutral or uninformed. Left to ourselves we "suppress the truth in unrighteousness" (Rom. 1:18 NASB). We know Paul's description for those outside of Christ to be true: "Since they did not think it worthwhile to retain the knowledge of God, he gave them over to a depraved mind . . ." (Rom. 1:28).

The confidence that we have in the Bible to tell us the truth and to correct the false thinking of our minds inspires the attention given to the Scriptures in the Reformed community. In sermons that expound the Bible and in classes that study the Bible in a variety of ways, we seek to have our misunderstandings challenged and changed. We also study the catechism and other doctrinal summaries of the Bible, not as a supplement to the Bible or as an authority equal to it, but because they connect us with centuries of biblical study by faithful Reformed teachers who have gone before us. We share in the wisdom of the church of all ages. We do not believe that any one Christian can independently understand all of God's revelation. We cannot come to sound doctrine if we know the teachers and preachers of only our day. We try to profit from the study of all those who have loved the Word of God and sought to submit to its teachings.

The disciplines of action connect, of course, with the disciplines of the mind. Action is needed to participate in worship and study. But Christian discipline goes beyond study. Action gives expression to the reality of new life in Christ. As Paul wrote, "You were taught . . . to be made new in the attitude of your minds; and to put on the new self, created to be like God in true righteousness and holiness" (Eph. 4:22–24). That new self showed God's children to be "children of light" (Eph. 5:8) who are dedicated to living "a life of love, just as Christ loved us and gave himself up for us as a fragrant offering and sacrifice to God" (Eph. 5:2).

That new life includes actions of piety and devotion. But it also involves fellowship that shows the love and care of God's people for one another. It involves service of many kinds—

teaching, comforting, visiting, counseling, cooking, and cleaning—both for the congregation and for those outside the household of faith. It also involves giving of time and talents to help those with many different kinds of needs. Giving involves sacrificial contributions of money to provide for the local ministry of the church and for ministries beyond it. As I came to know of all the works supported by the rather small denomination of which our congregation was a part—the schools, colleges and seminaries, retirement homes, missionaries at home and abroad, as well as local ministry—I was amazed. Truly remarkable disciplines of action were practiced.

Finally, we can think of the disciplines of time. When Paul told Christians to be very careful how they live, he went on: "redeeming the time, because the days are evil" (Eph. 5:16 NKJV). Exactly because we live in evil, degenerate times, time is important. The Christian must buy back the right time (this is the word-for-word translation of the phrase that the NIV rather weakly renders "making the most of every opportunity"). The Christian wants to avoid the lament of Shakespeare's Richard II: "I wasted time, now doth time waste me." We want to use time faithfully and effectively.

The disciplines of time mean that there is time for God and time with God. They mean time for God's people and with God's people. They mean time for service to the needs of the world according to our callings.

I soon discovered in my new church that time revolved around one day a week for God, Sunday as the Christian Sabbath. Long before I thought carefully about whether the Bible actually taught that Sunday was a Sabbath in the New Covenant, I fell into that pattern of living. I really looked forward to Sunday school, two worship services, and then Young People's Society. I enjoyed the fellowship, the worship, and the

45

learning. I liked the weekly rhythm that the Sabbath brought to my life.

It was not always easy for me to follow the pattern of the Sabbath. My parents were not always sympathetic. They often took the family out to dinner on Sunday night and were unhappy when I said that I would rather go to church. They feared that I was getting connected with a cult. I joked with them that I was the only kid in town who got in trouble for going to church too much. My father once remarked that perhaps they should not worry too much, since he and my mother had been raised in the Methodist Church with the same attitudes toward the Sabbath.

I did not really understand the practice of the Sabbath in those early days. I remember the first Sunday I spent with the Hoekenga family in the afternoon. After a delicious dinner, the parents headed off for a nap. That left four of us to occupy ourselves, and I suggested that we play bridge. This suggestion was greeted with some consternation—which I did not understand at the time. I suspect that some consultation was needed with Mom and Dad. Finally some cards were found, and I spent some time trying to teach bridge to three young people who knew nothing about cards. I am sure that it was a guilty time for them—cards on Sunday!—but they were trying to be hospitable to the uninformed outsider among them.

Two or more generations ago, the Reformed view of the Sabbath was not as strange as it seems to many today. Most American Protestants believed that Sunday was the Christian Sabbath. Today that Sabbath idea has all but disappeared except in Reformed and Presbyterian churches. Who is right about the Sabbath? How is the Sabbath to be observed? What does the Bible say?

The book of Revelation is full of intriguing and mysterious images and passages. My interest, however, is in a seemingly incidental and obvious phrase in chapter 1. John records that he received his commission to write and his first vision "on the Lord's Day" (Rev. 1:10). What exactly does John mean by "the Lord's Day"? And how does this day relate to the worship of God?

The word "Lord's" in this text is a rather unusual one in the New Testament. In pagan literature it occurs more frequently and means "imperial," that is, belonging to the emperor. In the New Testament it occurs only in 1 Corinthians 11:20 in addition to Revelation 1:10. In 1 Corinthians the word is used of the Lord's Supper, the unique meal among meals that belongs to the Lord in a special way as a sacrament of the body and blood of Jesus Christ. But is there a day in the New Covenant that belongs as uniquely to the Lord as the Lord's Supper does?

In today's Christian churches, many voices are heard to insist that all days are alike under the New Covenant. They appeal to Paul's words in Romans 14:5: "One man regards one day above another, another regards every day alike. Let each man be fully convinced in his own mind" (NASB). They also appeal to Galatians 4:10–11: "You observe days and months and seasons and years. I fear for you, that perhaps I have labored over you in vain" (NASB). But the context of Paul's words in both cases is the danger of Judaizing. In Romans 14 Paul is discussing foods as well as days. I believe that he is discussing the Jewish dietary laws and the Jewish calendar of holidays and saying that Christians are free either to observe or to do away with such arrangements of the Old Covenant. Paul is not speaking abstractly about days. He is arguing that Christians are not bound to observe the special days of the Old

Covenant. Paul's words do not contradict John's teaching that there is a day that belongs in a special way to the Lord in the New Covenant.

Could this Lord's Day, then, be the seventh-day Sabbath of the Jews? Groups such as the Seventh-Day Adventists answer in the affirmative. They rightly note—as the Reformed did before them—that the Sabbath is not just a Mosaic institution, but a creation ordinance and a picture of the consummation (Heb. 4). May not the seventh-day Sabbath then be the Lord's Day? But this idea is clearly rejected by Paul. For Paul, the seventh-day Sabbath is fulfilled in Christ. He wrote, "Therefore let no one act as your judge in regard to food or drink or in respect to a festival or a new moon or a Sabbath day—things which are a mere shadow of what is to come; but the substance belongs to Christ" (Col. 2:16–17 NASB).

If the "Lord's Day" of Revelation 1:10 shows us that there is a special day that belongs to the Lord in the New Covenant, and if Paul tells us that the Sabbath is fulfilled in Christ, then what day is the Lord's Day? Some few have argued that it is Easter, that is, an annual commemoration of Christ's resurrection. But does such an idea have any support in the New Testament? No. The New Testament hints at no annual celebrations of any kind.

Are we then left to conclude that John's reference to the "Lord's Day" is simply inexplicable? Are there any other options with biblical support left? When we look carefully at the New Testament, we find that a day is singled out for special attention: *the first day of the week*. In addition to the references to the resurrection of Jesus on the first day, there are references to meetings with Jesus and acts of worship on the first day in John 20:26, Acts 2:1, Acts 20:7, and 1 Corinthians 16:2. Since the first day of the week is the only day of the week, month, or year that gets any special notice in the New Testament, it must be the Lord's Day. Only seeing Sunday as the Lord's Day brings all the pieces of New Testament revelation into harmony.

By this time you may be wondering, "Didn't we know that already?" Well, many of us believed it already. But in my experience, many of us have begun to waver, doubting whether the Bible really tells us that Sunday is the Lord's Day. One hundred or even fifty years ago, the sanctity of the Lord's Day was an undoubted doctrine not only among Reformed people, but also among Methodists, Baptists, Episcopalians, Congregationalists, and many others. But today when so many, even among Bible-believing evangelicals, insist that there is no special day in the New Covenant, we need to read our Bibles closely again and to be renewed in our conviction that Sunday is indeed the Lord's Day.

When we recognize that Sunday is the Lord's Day, we begin to see a beautiful element of God's redemptive work in human history. We see how the seventh-day Sabbath pointed forward to rest that would come at the end of work. The Lord's Day on the first day of the week points to rest already won in Christ. The Lord's Day—the day that belongs in a unique way to Jesus—is a special day for worship and fellowship with Jesus. It is the weekly day to assemble together to encourage one another as we celebrate the resurrection of Jesus. It is the time for communal worship when, through the person and work of Jesus, we enter the heavenly temple to enjoy the presence and blessing of God (Heb. 10). It is the day to rest from ordinary activities to acknowledge God as the source and center of our lives. There is a day that belongs to Jesus in a special way. Revelation 1:10 is a key to knowing that Sunday is the Lord's Day. That Christian Sabbath has been a great blessing of rest and worship for me.

Promises

ROMANS 5 : 1 - 2 1

My entry into the life of the church was remarkably easy and enjoyable. What I learned from sermons and studies seemed perfectly true and reasonable to me. But for months I wondered whether I was really a Christian or not. I had heard a variety of expressions about what it meant to become a Christian: repentance, conversion, being born again, believing in Jesus, and having a personal relationship with Jesus. I accepted that I was a sinner because the Bible said so, but I was not sure that I felt sorry enough for my sin, or even felt particularly like a sinner. I knew that I had changed attitudes and behavior, but I did not feel radically different. I believed, but I had learned enough to know that there was a difference between assenting to truth and actually having saving faith. I was not sure which kind of faith I had.

I was particularly unsettled by the call to have a personal relationship with Jesus. All the Christians I knew seemed to assume that this was an easy idea to understand, and all seemed

51

to have that relationship. I knew what a personal relationship was. I was a shy person in high school, but I had family and friends with whom I had personal relationships. With family and friends a relationship meant conversation, physical proximity, doing things together—all sorts of things that did not seem to be true of my relationship with Jesus. I knew that I could talk to him in prayer and that he spoke to me through his Word. I knew that he was always present with me by his Spirit. But that still seemed somehow short of a "personal relationship," as I understood it. I felt that there must be something wrong with me and the kind of faith I had.

As a newcomer to a Reformed church and as someone who had always been interested in history, I began to learn more about the Reformation and John Calvin. I saw that for the Reformers, faith was understood as trusting the promises of Jesus. That definition of *faith* made real sense to me. Both *trust* and *promise* were clear terms. I began to think about the words of Jesus, "Come to Me, all who are weary and heavy-laden, and I will give you rest" (Matt. 11:28 NASB). Here was a clear promise from Jesus: I will give you rest. I will be your Savior. This promise is directed to all those who know they are in trouble: the weary and heavy-laden. All the sinner has to do is come. Here is where I had a problem. I wanted to come. I thought maybe I had come. But I was not sure that I had come in the right way, that I was sincere enough or sorry enough.

Gradually I began to see my predicament in terms that today I would call more genuinely Reformed. I realized that in my agonizing I had been focusing on myself and my doing. I had thought I was being Reformed by telling myself that I could not come to Jesus except by the grace of God and that I did not know whether I had received that grace. But then I began to understand that I was thinking in a self-centered way.

I was not really thinking about Jesus. Indeed, I was really saying that he was a liar. He said, "Come," and I said, "I can't come." He said, "I will give you rest," and I said, "You haven't given me rest." I finally concluded that it was not in fact virtuous or pious to treat Jesus as a liar. *Trust* meant precisely that I would rely completely on the word of Jesus as revealed in the Bible. As I looked less at myself and more at Jesus, I came to have peace in him.

That peace is what Paul saw as the effect of justification when he wrote: "Therefore, since we have been justified through faith, we have peace with God through our Lord Jesus Christ, through whom we have gained access by faith into this grace in which we now stand" (Rom. 5:1–2).

After Paul had concluded his most detailed discussion of justification in Romans 3 and 4, he declared that therefore we have peace with God. What is that peace? In some parts of the world, *peace* may mean the end of armed conflict even though the old hatreds and armaments remain. This situation is not so much peace as a cease-fire. Or *peace* may refer to a situation such as that of the American sector in Berlin after World War II. Fighting had stopped, arms were laid down and hatreds abandoned (by Germans thankful that they were not in the Russian sector), but only devastation and rubble marked the reality of life after peace. Paul has something much more positive in mind when he thinks of peace in Romans 5:1. He thinks of the "way of peace," a phrase from Isaiah 59:8 that Paul quoted in Romans 3:17. For Isaiah, the way of peace stands for holiness, love, justice, integrity, truth, contentment, and righteousness. It is the straight, smooth path of life with a loving and redeeming God, in contrast with the crooked path of the wicked.

In the immediate context of the book of Romans, Paul contrasts peace with the just punishment for sin (Rom. 3:25) that God in his wrath would visit upon the wicked (Rom. 4:5). The reality of sin and the reality of God's justice and holiness are essential elements of a Christian outlook on the world. One of the tragedies of so much contemporary church life is that the truth about the holiness of God and his wrath against sin has all but disappeared from view. In an effort to "connect" with contemporary non-Christians, the church has given much of its energy to teaching adjustment and self-acceptance. The implication of this teaching is that the great human need is to have peace with yourself. But such a view is far from the biblical revelation and from true Christianity.

In a Christian view of reality, the first need of the human heart is not to feel good, but to find peace with a holy and righteous God. The first function of the law in a fallen world is to teach sinners the sinfulness of sin (Rom. 3:20) and to teach that those lost in sin do not know the way of peace (Rom. 3:17). Sinners as violators of God's holy law have no peace with God because they are not righteous. The righteous God can have peace only with the righteous. Paul has warned sinners, however, that "there is no one righteous, not even one" (Rom. 3:10).

For sinners to be reconciled to God, therefore, a new righteousness and a new way to righteousness is needed. Paul makes that clear: "But now a righteousness from God, apart from law, has been made known. . . . This righteousness from God comes through faith in Jesus Christ to all who believe" (Rom. 3:21–22). The peace in which Paul rejoices is the peace of sin covered, wrath averted, and justice satisfied. That peace comes from the righteousness found only in Jesus, in his life and death.

Paul's reflections on peace as the fruit of justification may well depend in part on Isaiah 57. Of the contrite person God says, "I have seen his [sinful] ways, but I will heal him; I will guide him and restore comfort to him, creating praise on the lips of the mourners in Israel. Peace, peace, to those far and near . . ." (Isa. 57:18–19). But of the wicked he says, " 'There is no peace,' says my God, 'for the wicked' " (Isa. 57:21). The wicked are those who are indifferent to the covenant of the true God and have formed a false righteousness for themselves. God says of them, "Whom have you so dreaded and feared that you have been false to me, and have neither remembered me nor pondered this in your hearts? Is it not because I have long been silent that you do not fear me? I will expose your righteousness and your works, and they will not benefit you" (Isa. 57:11–12).

In the years I have lived since gaining peace in Jesus, I have come more and more to appreciate the words of John Calvin as one of the clearest and truest interpreters of God's Word. In his commentary on Romans 5, Calvin explains this peace as the believer's "serenity of conscience, which originates from the awareness of having God reconciled to himself." Notice how Calvin has highlighted the objective and subjective dimensions of the peace. Objectively, peace with God means that God is in fact reconciled to us because of the saving work of Christ for us. Subjectively, peace with God means that we come to know and experience that God is reconciled to us and that this knowledge brings us serenity in our consciences that would otherwise accuse and condemn us. The union of these objective and subjective elements is the glorious peace enjoyed by the children of God.

On the objective side, Jesus has done everything for us to win us that reconciliation with God. Paul presents the work of Christ for us in the comparison he develops between Jesus and

Adam in Romans 5. Adam brought sin into the world by his one transgression, and sin and death passed to all his posterity. Jesus came to save sinners from the result of Adam's disobedience and the sin that had brought death to the world (vv. 15–17). Christ faced a more demanding task than Adam, needing to overcome a world given over to death (v. 16). As Adam's one trespass brought condemnation, so Christ's one act of righteousness was justification (v. 18).

What was the one act of righteousness that Jesus performed? Since Paul frequently speaks of the death of Christ in Romans 3–5, some have suggested that the Savior's death on the cross was the one act of righteousness. Certainly the death of Christ is at the very heart and core of his saving work. But is it the totality of that work? Did Jesus only take away our sin, or did he also positively fulfill all the righteousness of the law for us so that we could stand confidently before God fully clothed in the righteousness of Christ? Paul made it clear that not only the death of Christ was saving, but also his life. Certainly his resurrected life is part and parcel of our salvation: "He was delivered over to death for our sins and was raised to life for our justification" (Rom. 4:25).

If we think carefully about Romans 5:18, we will see that Christ's one act of righteousness must be more than his death on the cross alone. We must recognize that the dying of the Savior for sins is a whole series of acts. He is quiet in the face of the false judgment. He is comforting to his disciples and the one thief on the cross. He suffers the full measure of the wrath of God against sin. He declares that his atoning work is finished. The sacrificial work of Christ is many acts, not one. Indeed, the Heidelberg Catechism makes it clear that the whole life of Christ was his suffering, not just the cross. Question 37 asks, "What does it mean that He *suffered?*" The answer: "That all the time He lived on earth, but especially at the end of His life, He bore, in body and soul, the wrath of God against the sin of the whole human race, in order that by His passion, as the only atoning sacrifice, He might redeem our body and soul from everlasting damnation and obtain for us the grace of God, righteousness, and eternal life."

So we come back to the question: what is the one act? Paul contrasts the one act of Adam's sin with the one act of Christ's righteousness. Adam's one act is easy to specify: breaking the command of God not to eat from the tree of the knowledge of good and evil. Christ's one act must then be his whole life of righteous obedience to all the commands of God. It is only by the integrity of that whole life, the seamless wholeness of his obedience, that he accomplished salvation. His entire life was one act of righteousness. By that one act, he both takes away our sin by the cross and credits his righteousness to us.

Paul tells us that God "will credit righteousness—for us who believe in him" (Rom. 4:24). That righteousness is the righteousness of Jesus. Jesus fulfilled the law, not just for himself, but also for us so that our reconciliation means that we stand before God with all of Christ's law-keeping reckoned to our account. As Calvin put it, "When . . . we come to Christ, we first find in Him the exact righteousness of the law, and this also becomes ours by imputation" (on Rom. 3:21).

Imputation is a critical word for understanding Paul and biblical religion. It means crediting or reckoning something to someone. For the Christian, it means that the work of Christ is credited to him. This crediting is crucial because it means that the full and perfect work of Christ is applied to the believer in the divine economy. Some forms of theology, such as the Roman Catholic view, stress the infusion of Christ's righteousness into the believer instead of imputation. A theology of infusion teaches that the righteousness of Christ is put into the believer, making him more righteous in reality. The problem with such a theology in relation to justification is that it does not acknowledge that such a righteousness put into the believer will never be full and perfect. The minute I receive the righteousness of Christ in me, I pollute it by my sinfulness. It cannot then be the perfect righteousness I need. But when the righteousness of Christ is credited to me outside of me, then it remains perfect and provides me with salvation.

Again when we look to the Heidelberg Catechism, we find this understanding of the work of Christ. The catechism makes it clear that he obtained righteousness for us by his life of obedience and imputes that righteousness to us. The Reformed have always maintained such an understanding of peace with God. Question 60 asks one of the critical, central questions of Christianity: "How are you righteous before God?" The answer is: "Only by a true faith in Jesus Christ; that is, though my conscience accuse me that I have grievously sinned against all the commandments of God and kept none of them, and am still inclined to all evil, yet God, without any merit of mine, of mere grace, grants and imputes to me the perfect satisfaction, righteousness, and holiness of Christ, as if I had never had nor committed any sin, and myself had accomplished all the obedience which Christ has rendered for me; if only I accept such benefit with a believing heart." I am as righteous in the sight of God as if I had accomplished all the obedience that Christ rendered for me. What a foundation for a certain and secure relationship with a righteous God!

On the subjective side, such serenity or peace is missed, Calvin argues, by two sorts of persons. The first sort are those whose consciences are still filled with fear and a sense of God's anger with them as sinners. "No one will stand without fear before God, unless he relies on free reconciliation, for as long as God is judge, all men must be filled with fear and confusion. . . . Wretched souls are always uneasy, unless they rest in the grace of Christ" (on Rom. 5:1). Such people either do not understand the work of Christ in its fullness and completeness or have not rightly understood the gospel's implications for themselves. If they miss the completeness of Christ's work, they are filled with fear because they think they have failed to augment what is lacking in the work of Christ. Such people demean Christ by thinking to add their works to his without realizing that such an addition is always a subtraction (like adding a mustache to the Mona Lisa). All who deny that we are saved by grace alone are guilty of this error. Others do not grasp that the full benefit of Christ's work is theirs by faith alone. They are like hypochondriacs—who, although healthy, do not enjoy their healthy state. They are in constant doubt about their relationship to God and do not know the confidence that should characterize the Christian life. They are like the mother who said to her son, "O, that we might die tonight, so that we would not sin and fall from grace tomorrow."

The second sort who fail to experience the peace of Christ, according to Calvin, are those who see no danger for themselves. "This serenity is possessed neither by the Pharisee, who is inflated by a false confidence in his works, nor by a senseless sinner, who, since he is intoxicated with the pleasure of his vices, feels no lack of peace. . . . Peace with God is opposed to the drunken security of the flesh. . . ." Here again are two sorts of people. The former are actually secure in believing that their works are good enough to gain them some claim on the divine goodness. They utterly fail to realize that even their best works are flawed in God's sight. The latter—perhaps the majority in our world—have no sense at all of any danger from the wrath of God. They are like the dying man who, when asked if he had made his peace with God, responded that he did not know that they had quarreled.

The only true antidote to fear and to self-satisfaction is faith. Faith is that trust in Christ and his work that looks away from all the valid grounds in ourselves for fear and away from all the vain flattery of self-satisfaction. Faith alone looks to Christ alone, and Christ alone justifies those who have faith alone.

The tragedy of the contemporary evangelical tendency toward fuzziness on or even to betrayal of the Protestant doctrine of justification should now be clear. Justification is neither some irrelevant squabble over technical bits of theology nor a doctrine subordinate to Christian cooperation and activity. The doctrine of justification determines the way in which we understand the gospel we have to preach, the legitimate bounds of cooperation, and the motivation for good works. When the biblical doctrine of justification is not kept pure, the work of Christ is robbed of its meaning and glory and the Christian forfeits true peace with God.

Again we can listen to Calvin as he joins the objective and subjective dimensions of our peace with God: "We see now how the righteousness of faith is the righteousness of Christ. When, therefore, we are justified, the efficient cause is the mercy of God, Christ is the substance (*materia*) of our justification, and the Word, with faith, the instrument. Faith is therefore said to justify, because it is the instrument by which we receive Christ, in whom righteousness is communicated to us" (on Rom. 3:31). Here is the true peace that I came to know as I grew to understand Paul and his faithful interpreter John Calvin. Already in high school I was beginning to learn how the Reformation could help a young Christian grow in faith and understanding.

Certainty

EPHESIANS 1 : 1 - 2 3

My personal struggles with faith had led me to look to the wisdom of the Reformation for help and guidance in understanding the Bible. My interest in history was now linked to my theological interests and concerns. It was the beginning of a lifetime of study largely related to sixteenth- and seventeenth-century history.

My interest in the Reformation grew during my years as an undergraduate at Stanford University (1963–1967). I had briefly considered majoring in political science but soon realized that such a discipline was too abstract for me. I pursued instead my earlier interests in history with all its concreteness and uniqueness. History has always seemed to me a very humane discipline.

Taking the course on Reformation history taught by Lewis Spitz is one of my fondest memories of those undergraduate years. At that time I knew that Spitz was one of the most popular teachers on campus, but I did not realize then that he was one of the most respected Reformation scholars in the world. He was a particular expert on the relationship between the influence of the Renaissance in Germany and the rise of Luther and Lutheranism. Part of Spitz's appeal as a lecturer was his remarkable sense of humor. Every lecture began with almost five minutes of jokes and wry remarks. I never heard him repeat a joke.

He was also a wonderfully clear lecturer. He wrote a brief outline on the blackboard at the beginning of each class and followed it, finishing each presentation in perfect harmony with the bell signaling the end of the period. His lectures were the product of great learning, presented with no notes—except for the outline and a pocketful of index cards on which were written quotations that he read from time to time. Sometimes he read in English, but more often initially in Latin or German, which he would then translate. Once in a long while, he would just read the Latin, look up, smile, and say, "You Stanford students think you are so smart; figure it out for yourselves."

His lectures on Luther's theology I found profoundly moving. They were a careful and faithful presentation of what Luther had believed. But they also expressed Spitz's personal commitments. He was a loyal son of the Lutheran Church–Missouri Synod. His father had taught church history and systematic theology at Concordia Seminary in St. Louis, and the Spitz family had supported J.A.O. Preus in his defense of confessional orthodoxy in the church. Spitz's lectures greatly deepened my understanding of and love for Reformation theology.

If Spitz's teaching had any weakness, it was on Calvin and Calvinism. He was not as familiar with Calvin as with Luther and tended to accept some of the traditional Lutheran generalizations about the Reformed. His careful exposition of Luther helped me to see how much Luther and Calvin had in common and also to see some areas of difference between them—for example, on the sacraments, the church, and the Christian life.

As I have studied the development of Calvinist thought, one of the themes that has impressed me over and over is that of certainty. This theme emerged clearly in the writings of Calvin himself and has been maintained by Calvinism at its best ever since.

Certainty manifests itself at several points in Reformed thought. First, there is the certainty that the Bible is the Word of God. That confidence is the firm foundation on which Reformed theology has been built. Second, there is the certainty that the believer can know that he is saved. The doubts and fears that dominated Christian attitudes in the Middle Ages gave way in the Reformation to assurance that God surely accepts the believer in Christ. These two points of certainty are common to both Lutheran and Reformed heirs of the Reformation.

Calvinism, however, added a remarkable third certainty—that the believer was one of God's elect and would persevere in faith to the end. Here Reformed and Lutherans parted company. Lutheran theology confessed a doctrine of election, but saw it as part of the realm of the hidden will of God and not a revealed part of the life of grace for the Christian. Calvinists integrated election into the life of grace. They rejected any idea that election threatened or darkened the Christian's experience of grace. They followed the path of Paul in Ephesians 1, where he rejoices in the doctrine of election and in deriving comfort from it.

Where Reformed theology was distinctive, it was also often attacked. Not only was it criticized from without by Roman Catholics and Lutherans, but in the early seventeenth century it was attacked from within by a movement that became known as Arminianism. Named after James Arminius, a minister in the Dutch Reformed Church, Arminianism became influential in the history of the church, influencing most Methodist and Pentecostal theologies. The Arminians summarized their challenge to Reformed orthodoxy in five points: (1) that election to eternal life was conditional on faith and obedience, (2) that Christ had died for all individuals on the cross, (3) that all individuals were completely and helplessly lost in sin, (4) that God's grace to rescue sinners from their sin was resistible, and (5) that it was unclear whether those regenerated by the grace of God could lose that grace and be finally lost.

Much confusion has arisen from the tendency of the Reformed to talk of the five points of Calvinism. Such talk implies that Calvinism is simply summarized in five points. In reality, Calvinism cannot be reduced to five points, but is summarized only in its confessions, such as the Belgic Confession, the Heidelberg Catechism, and the Westminster Confession. But in its fullness, Calvinism does have five answers to the five errors of Arminianism: the five points of Calvinism.

The orthodox Reformed response to the challenge of Arminianism became a special interest of mine when I returned to Stanford (1970–1974) for doctoral study with Dr. Spitz. While studying Renaissance and Reformation history generally, I began to focus on early-seventeenth-century Dutch Calvinism. I would finally spend two years in such study, with particular attention on the orthodox Reformed theologians' various opinions on the atoning work of Christ.

Taken together, the so-called five points of Calvinism are often called the doctrines of grace. For Calvinists, those five points all reinforce the gracious character of salvation and are vital to the full sense of certainty and assurance that Calvinists—indeed, all Christians—should enjoy. And for Calvinists, these points are not the deductions of theology but rather the clear teaching of the Bible. While we cannot take time to show the full biblical evidence that proves these doctrines, we can see strong support for them in the opening verses of Paul's letter to the Ephesians. Paul begins by identifying himself as an apostle, speaking words of blessing on the saints of God, and praising God for his grace and goodness in Christ. He goes on to celebrate the doctrines of grace, particularly the theme of election or predestination. Like Romans 8, Ephesians 1 provides us with a golden chain of blessings from the Lord in which predestination is a crucial link.

Paul in Ephesians 1 not only teaches us something of the content of the doctrines of grace, but also teaches us how to speak about them. He speaks so naturally, so easily, so confidently about them that he teaches us also how to speak. He does not analyze every aspect of these doctrines in Ephesians 1, but he does show us something of what to speak, when to speak, and why to speak of them.

WHAT TO SPEAK

Paul begins his letter by celebrating God's action in choosing "us"—his own people—for salvation. Paul writes that God blesses his saints with every spiritual blessing (Eph. 1:3), that God chose us to be holy (v. 4), and that he predestined us to be adopted as his children (v. 5). God clearly chooses us to salvation in Christ. But on what basis? Does God choose us to salvation on the basis of something in us or only on the basis of his own will?

Paul's answer is clear throughout these verses. First, he says that God chose us "before the foundation of the world" (Eph. 1:4 NASB). Since he chose us before we were, that certainly implies that the reason for choosing us is in God, not in us.

Second, Paul says that we are chosen in accordance with God's pleasure and will (Eph. 1:5). Paul uses the same word for "will" here that he used in verse 1 to describe himself as an apostle by the will of God. Calvin called Paul a mirror of election. As Paul was sovereignly chosen to be an apostle, so we are sovereignly chosen to salvation. Paul was not chosen because of his superior goodness, but only because of God's merciful will.

Third, Paul says that we are chosen freely (Eph. 1:6). God is free in election. He is not moved or compelled by anything external to himself. He chooses freely in accordance with his good pleasure. God is utterly sovereign in election; his will, not ours, is determinative in salvation. Paul says nothing here about human free will as a factor in election or salvation. In fact, nowhere in the Bible is the phrase "free will" to be found. The idea of free will is never used as a factor in the salvation of sinners.

God is always at the center of biblical discussions of election and salvation. The Bible calls us to be radically God-centered in our thinking. The doctrine of election is a crucial way to keep us theocentric.

Fourth, Paul says that we are chosen in Jesus Christ (Eph. 1:5), in the one God loves (v. 6). God does not love us in ourselves and on our own; he loves us only in Christ, the one who deserves his love. In Christ we are adopted as sons (v. 5), and only in Christ do we have every spiritual blessing (v. 3). The eternal plan of God to save the elect is brought to effect in the death of Christ for the elect. Ephesians 1 does not explicitly state that Christ died only for the elect (for that teaching see, for example, Matt. 20:28; 26:28; John 10:15). Paul does clarify in Ephesians, however, that the electing plan of the Father is not separate from the Son, but very much in and with the Son (Eph. 1:6–7, 9–11).

Paul also relates the Holy Spirit to the work of grace in the lives of his people. The Spirit is the one who gives us the blessing of Christ and seals us as those belonging to Christ (Eph. 1:13–14, 17). This Spirit, Paul teaches, guarantees that we will inherit the fullness of the salvation that Christ has won for us (v. 17). Here at least in seed form are the doctrines of the irresistible work of the Spirit and his preserving us in the faith to the end.

WHEN TO SPEAK

When is it appropriate to speak of the doctrines of grace, and particularly of election? Even among those who believe in election, some seem to think that we should speak of predestination seldom, if ever. They treat election as our guilty secret—the less said, the better. Others believe that we should talk of election, but only with mature Christians. Election is a doctrine that should be introduced only to those already well grounded in the faith.

Both of these approaches to election assume that election is a problem. Why? Some say that it's because election is a mysterious and difficult doctrine. In some ways it is, but so is the Trinity. Yet no true Christian suggests that we ought to avoid teaching all Christians about the Trinity.

Others note that election is controversial and unpopular. But so is the doctrine of hell, and Christians have always felt a responsibility to make clear the reality of final judgment.

Still others say that election is a problem because it can so easily be misrepresented. Yet that is true of nearly every other Christian doctrine as well. The evangelical doctrine of justification, for example, has often been misrepresented as leading to an indifference to holy Christian living. Even so, we continue to believe that we must teach that we are justified by grace alone through faith alone.

Election has often been misrepresented—and not only by those who reject it. Some have twisted the doctrine of predestination into a kind of fatalism and an excuse for a lack of concern with evangelism. One such group, known in the nineteenth century as Hard-Shell Baptists, even wrote hymns misusing the doctrine of election. One such hymn, whose words I heard quoted in a speech by the Baptist church historian Timothy George, proclaims:

> We are God's elected few;
> Let all the rest be damned.
> There's room enough in Hell for you.
> We don't want Heaven crammed.

Such arrogant indifference to evangelism is completely foreign to the genuine character of the Reformed doctrines of grace.

A final reason why some see election as a problem—perhaps the most important reason—is that election strikes many as being unfair. Yet ordinary human standards of fairness conflict with several other elements of Christian revelation. The doctrines of original sin and total depravity strike many as unfair, but are clearly taught in Scripture and are essential to the structure of Christian theology. The doctrine of the imputation of Christ's righteousness to sinners is not "fair," but is at the very heart of the gospel. Election may not always or fully seem fair from our human perspective, but it is foundational to God's mercy to sinners.

The effect of not talking about election in the contemporary church has been disastrous. Today religion tends to be more man-centered than medieval Christianity before the Reformation. At least in the Middle Ages the stress on human ability was focused on overcoming sin and meriting eternal life. Today in too many churches the focus is on using one's human potential to gain health, wealth, and happiness. This man-centeredness is found even in many churches that consider themselves evangelical.

When we compare the modern church's relative silence about election with the Bible, we find that the Bible speaks frequently and frankly about predestination. If we want to be biblical, we too must talk about it. And we must do so with the biblical confidence that election is a solution, not a problem. Election is the solution because it glorifies God at every point in salvation and draws us away from ourselves to God.

We must, of course, speak of election in a clear, sensitive, and careful manner. As John Calvin said in a sermon on Ephesians 1: "We know that our wisdom ought always to begin with humility." But our humility should not lead us to silence. Rather, it should lead us to imitate Paul in his joyous expression of God's electing love.

Why to Speak

Paul speaks of election because it glorifies God (Eph. 1:6). Election glorifies God because it shows that at every point salvation is God's work. He originates the plan of salvation in eternity. He elects specific sinners whom his Spirit will bring to faith in his Son.

The glory of his saving work leads us to praise God. Our minds in the first place should not focus on our needs or our strengths, but should break into thanksgiving to God for all he has done. As Paul begins the letter to the Ephesians with a long prayer of praise, so praise and adoration should feature prominently in our lives. As Calvin so powerfully says in his sermon, "All who would do away with God's predestination or are loathe to hear it spoken of, thereby show themselves to be mortal enemies of God's praise."

We should also speak of election because it is a constituent part of our assurance of salvation. Election reminds us that any grace that is present in us comes from God and that God will complete in us the work that he has begun. If we are in Christ, it is because we are elect. We know we are elect and are strengthened in faith by contemplating Jesus. Again as Calvin said in his sermon on Ephesians 1:4–6, "Jesus Christ is the mirror in which God beholds us when he wishes to find us acceptable to himself. Likewise, on our side, he is the mirror on which we must cast our eyes and look, when we desire to come to the knowledge of our election." Those most sure of their election in Christ are those who can say with the most understanding and passion: "Jesus saves!"

Today Reformed believers are tempted to see their doctrine of election as a peculiarity, almost as a sectarian notion. We must remember that in the history of the church great theologians from Augustine to Thomas Aquinas to Martin Luther as well as the many Reformed theologians have believed in predestination. Reformed theology has incorporated that biblical and historic doctrine of election as one of the doctrines of grace central to Christian life. The doctrines of grace are glorious truths of God's Word with great practical importance for the life of individual Christians and of the church. Let us continue to be biblical and speak freely of God's gracious saving work. And let us live with the wonderful certainty that he who began a good work in us will bring it to completion in the day of Christ Jesus (Phil. 1:6).

Always More

COLOSSIANS 1 : 1 - 14

Reformed Christianity seemed to fit well with my interests and needs as a studious high school student. Still quite shy and often feeling that I didn't know what to say, I tended to enjoy books more than people. In part, books were a form of escape to interesting worlds that I could observe without speaking. In part books were intellectually stimulating. I liked the new events, places, and ideas found in books.

I soon discovered that Calvinism had a rich history and a great intellectual heritage. I know now that Calvinism, especially in America, has sometimes been too exclusively seen as a faith only for thinkers and theologians. But the Reformed faith is much more than just a religion of the head. I certainly experienced from the beginning the warmth, the piety, the hospitality, and the deep sense of community to be found in Reformed churches. Calvinism is knowledge, but it is also the eager pursuit of holiness and loving service in the church and in the world.

Still, the intellectual side of the faith was very important to me. I eagerly pursued both the biblical–theological side of the faith and the history of Calvinism in high school and in college. As my college days drew to an end in 1967, I was uncertain about my future. Finally I decided to go to seminary after college—primarily to study rather than to prepare for the ministry.

Which seminary to attend became the new problem for me. A classmate, Robert Johnston, was heading for Fuller Seminary in Pasadena and urged me to join him there. I visited the campus and enjoyed the welcome of his parents and others there, but I did not feel particularly drawn to Fuller. I knew that the Christian Reformed Church had its own seminary in Grand Rapids, Michigan, and some of my friends from the church in Alameda recommended Westminster Seminary in Philadelphia. I was unsure what to do.

Several times I spoke with two of the ministers at the Presbyterian church that I was attending in Menlo Park, California. Dr. Cary Weisiger and Dr. Clifford Smith had both graduated from Westminster Seminary, had served pastorates in the Orthodox Presbyterian Church, and were then in the United Presbyterian Church. Dr. Smith expressed reservations about the theological stability of some Fuller graduates he knew and thought that Westminster was perhaps too narrow. He recommended that I investigate Gordon Divinity School (which changed its name to Gordon-Conwell Theological Seminary during my third year there), located outside of Boston, where several fellow students from his Westminster days were teaching.

As I learned about Gordon, it seemed attractive. I thought that since I had lived all my life in California, it would be wise to study in another part of the country. (And as a committed northern Californian, I thought that Boston actually seemed less foreign than southern California.) I knew that Gordon was committed to the complete authority of the Bible and that Gordon had both Reformed and non-Reformed faculty members. I thought that since I had had all my exposure to Christianity in Reformed circles, it would be good for me to hear other points of view.

In retrospect, I believe that I would have gotten a more thorough and coherent education at Westminster, but in the providence of God Gordon was a very good place for me. I received a good education, became more convinced that Reformed Christianity was correct, and met three professors who had an especially strong influence on me. Dr. Meredith Kline introduced me to biblical theology and the importance of the covenant for an understanding of the work of Christ and the structure of the Bible. He encouraged my interest in the apologetics of Cornelius Van Til, arranging for Dr. Van Til to send me copies of many of his works. Dr. Kline, his wife Grace, and his oldest son Meredith (a friend and classmate at seminary) showed Mary Ellen and me great hospitality—including rescuing us from a snowstorm and giving us a place to stay for several days. Dr. Roger Nicole introduced me to the discipline of systematic theology and the splendors of the Canons of Dort. He generously tutored me in Latin and Dutch. He opened the great theological work of Herman Bavinck to me. Dr. Philip Edgcumbe Hughes reflected the urbane, witty, and broad dimensions of English scholarship with his remarkable achievements in New Testament studies, theology, and Reformation studies. He and his wife Margaret became my very close friends when we were colleagues on the faculty of Westminster in Philadelphia.

After seminary, I decided to undertake doctoral studies in Reformation history back at Stanford. Dr. Spitz became my adviser, and I had four quite wonderful years of study there, finishing my Ph.D. in 1974. While there, I had the opportunity to serve as a teaching assistant for two other great Reformation scholars: Dr. Wilhelm Pauck and Dr. Heiko Oberman. All three of these men not only were learned and personally encouraging, but were also inspiring teachers, bringing great passion to their lectures and seminars. I remember Dr. Pauck saying that the only reason for a lecture is to fire the imagination of the listener.

At each stage of my education, I found my faith growing. I certainly met ideas and individuals who attacked my faith— or were simply amazed at it. I remember meeting a young woman at Stanford my first week there as a freshman. When I told her that I was a Calvinist, she said, "Really! I thought they only existed in books." I never had a crisis of faith in all those years of study, but found that the Calvinism I had learned was able to grow with me and meet every challenge. Calvinism did not run from the world, but rather had the resources for understanding, evaluating, appreciating, and critiquing the ideas in that world.

My confidence in the intellectual viability and respectability of Calvinism was greatly helped by my acquaintance with the work of Cornelius Van Til. When I told my friends at the Alameda Christian Reformed Church that I was going to Stanford as an undergraduate, some of them were quite concerned. They believed that Christians should study at Christian colleges, and for a time I considered applying to Wheaton College. But my parents did not want me to go to a Christian college. (My mother after reading the Wheaton catalogue, with its prohibitions of dancing, movies, TV, drinking, and smoking, commented that the only thing left was sex.) So I was headed to Stanford. To help me prepare for the anti-Christian environment I would face there, a member of the church gave me a copy of Cornelius Van Til's book *Defense of the Faith*.

That book was one of the most useful gifts I ever received. As with Calvin's *Institutes*, I cannot claim that I read it all or understood it very fully. But I did learn two critical things from Van Til: first, that no person is neutral in his thinking, and second, that there are no brute facts. No person is neutral because every person has some kind of religious commitment. This religious commitment does not mean just what we think about God or doctrine. Rather, it refers to our ultimate ideas, values, and motives. It means that we all have fundamental presuppositions that color our ways of understanding our world. Even the skeptic who doubts everything has made doubt his ultimate standard. Doubt is the presupposition by which he evaluates everything. But at the deepest level he cannot prove the value of his doubt; rather, he believes it.

Because all thought is religious, Van Til rejects the notion of neutral or brute facts. By this he means that facts are always used in a context of interpretation. All the evidence used as proof of various ideas or systems of thought is in reality facts interpreted according to some religious system. Everyone uses facts according to his or her religious presuppositions.

Van Til's presuppositional approach to truth was very helpful to me as a young student in college. When my professors presented facts or ideas that challenged my faith, I did not have to feel that unless I immediately had answers to those challenges, my faith might begin to waver. Rather, I knew that the professors challenged my faith from a faith commitment of their own, and the facts they presented reflected the interpretive context of their religious commitment. I was not surprised that I could not always answer them, because they were better educated and more experienced than I was. Van Til helped me to feel comfortable saying, "I don't know."

Let me give an example. As a freshman at Stanford, I took a course in the history of Western civilization in which we studied the story of creation in Genesis. The professor commented that there were two creation stories in Genesis 1 and Genesis 2 that contradicted each other. He taught this contradiction as a fact. At that time I did not know all that I would later learn about Genesis. But I did know that as I read Genesis 1 and 2, I could see no contradictions. I also knew that my professor interpreted Genesis according to his own religious presuppositions: namely, (1) that the Bible was not the revelation of God, (2) that Moses had not written Genesis, but that it was a collection of many authors' writing over many years, and (3) that these many authors had contradictory ideas that had not been entirely harmonized when Genesis was put together. None of these presuppositions were neutral facts, but all expressed the religious or intellectual positions of my professor. By recognizing those presuppositions, I could evaluate his teaching without anxiety. I did not need to have a "fact" to answer every one of his "facts" (although there are plenty of facts to support the Christian position). I could accept the limits of my knowledge at 18 without feeling that my faith was weakened.

Some of Van Til's critics have accused him of promoting an anti-intellectual spirit that is indifferent to the ideas and evidences of other religions. They say that he does not really encourage thinking, but only irrational commitment. I do not think that criticism is fair. Van Til did say that we can never know everything as God knows everything. Our very creaturely limitations should humble our confidence in the powers of our minds. But Van Til entered into vigorous scholarly discussion with other points of view, trying to help others see how their ideas were inconsistent or not very self-conscious about their starting points. He took their ideas and facts seriously and sought to show how the best ideas and the facts, rightly understood, supported the Christian faith as revealed in the Bible.

The Reformed Christianity that I learned was not fearful of the world or eager to hide from the challenges of the day. Rather, it was confident that the mind should be used as a servant of true religion. We were indeed to love the Lord with all our minds. For two thousand years Christians had faced the attack of many different theologies, philosophies, and ideologies and had emerged stronger and more certain of the truth and intellectual integrity of their faith. As I studied, I had that same growing confidence.

This Reformed confidence that there are always more truths to learn and always more ways to grow in knowledge, holiness, and love is a thoroughly biblical idea. We can see that clearly in Paul's letter to the Colossians. Paul writes in the opening chapter about what those Christians already had in Christ and what they would yet grow to become in him.

The Colossians were already "holy and faithful" (Col. 1:2). They already had faith, love, and hope (vv. 4–5). They had already heard the gospel. They already understood the truth of God's grace (v. 6). They had already been rescued from the dominion of darkness and brought into the kingdom of the Son (v. 13). They already had redemption and the forgiveness of their sins (v. 14). Those Colossians had so much that we might be tempted to ask, what more could they have? Perhaps they might have been tempted to rest on their laurels.

In reality, however, chapter 2 of this letter shows us that they really did not appreciate how much they already had. They had fallen prey to teachers who told them that because they had so little, they had to adopt all sorts of difficult disciplines to be redeemed or to grow in Christ. They were told that they could not eat or touch certain things and that they had to worship in special ways—none of which God had taught in his Word.

Instead of growing in the truth of Christ, the Colossians had started to follow other teachings from other sources. They were following the principles of this world (2:8, 20), a reference to nature or to strange philosophies. They were following the traditions of men (2:8, 22), thinking that human wisdom could guide them in the service of God. They had misunderstood and were misusing the Old Testament (2:16–17), falling back into practices that had been fulfilled in Christ. They were following visions that claimed to be the revelations from angels about worship (2:18).

Paul, even before he warns the Colossians in chapter 2 of the dangers of these teachings, tells them in chapter 1 that they must still be learning and growing in the right way—namely, in Christ. He wants them to know that precisely because they already have so much, they must be growing even more. Paul wants to teach them that there is always more. There is always more to become and to do. He writes that their lives need to be developing so that those lives increasingly become worthy of the God who saved them (1:10). As Christians, they need to seek to please God in every way and to be growing in every good work (1:10). There ought to be a restlessness and dissatisfaction in every Christian life that we are not yet what we should be. We need to be eager and energetic, for example, in the pursuit of holiness. But real growth in holiness rests only on the foundation of the Father's work and Word (1:12). Neither our ability nor our cleverness can make us grow. Only God's power can do that (1:11).

This growth in holiness must rest on a growth in the knowledge of the truth. Colossians chapter 2 shows us that the Christians in Colossae had tried to grow in holiness through all kinds of practices that were not taught by God. Their knowledge was false and misguided. In order to grow in holiness, they had to grow in true knowledge of God's ways and will. That is why Paul tells them that he is praying for them that God would fill them with the knowledge of his will through all spiritual wisdom and understanding (1:9). They do not yet have all knowledge or all wisdom and understanding. They need to grow. There is always more to learn.

Paul wants to show them that all knowledge needs to be Christ-centered: "My purpose is that they may be encouraged in heart and united in love, so that they may have the full riches of complete understanding, in order that they may know the mystery of God, namely, Christ, in whom are hidden all the treasures of wisdom and knowledge" (2:2–3). As Christ is the only beginning for Christian living, so he is the only way to progress in the Christian life. "So then, just as you received Christ Jesus as Lord, continue to live in him, rooted and built up in him, strengthened in the faith as you were taught, and overflowing with thankfulness" (2:6–7). They needed Christ and his knowledge. They needed to continue in Christ as they had begun. They needed to build on what they had been taught by the apostle from the Word of truth.

Paul calls on them to reject false teachers and false paths, to return to Christ, and to build on what they had been taught. Christ and his Word are enough. We should always seek more knowledge, but we need to seek it in Christ and build on the foundation of his Word.

Since Paul's day, Christians have continued to struggle with the same issues that those early Christians faced. How do we grow in a way that really pleases Christ? How do we meet the ideas and challenges of the world?

Some Christians become anti-intellectual. They conclude that thinking and study are dangerous and ought to be avoided by Christians. They try to hide from the world and assume that there is nothing to learn from non-Christian thinkers. But such a position does not really love God with all the mind. It seeks to avoid conformity to the world not by the renewing of the mind, but by the closing of the mind. Paul studied the pagan writings of his day and quoted those authors to bolster his presentation of Christian truth (for example, Acts 17:28).

Other Christians have fallen into the opposite error. They have studied and embraced the thinking of this world too uncritically. They have accommodated their minds, rather than having their minds transformed. The rise of theological liberalism in many churches and schools is an example of that accommodation to non-Christian ideas.

The Reformed have always sought to be neither anti-intellectual nor accommodating intellectuals. They have tried neither to close their minds nor to hand their minds over to the ideas of the world. They have sought to grow in knowledge and understanding in Christ. For that reason, much of the best thinking and writing to present and defend the faith in recent centuries has come from Reformed authors.

I have spent about forty years studying the Bible and our Reformed heritage. I find it just as fulfilling and stimulating now as when I began. I also find that while I have learned much, there is always more to learn.

Callings

GENESIS 1 : 2 6 – 2 : 3

"How can you know God's will for your life?" I asked that question of some friends one day in the foyer of Frost Hall at Gordon-Conwell Theological Seminary. I was in my third year of study there and was uncertain about my future. Should I pursue ordination for the ministry, or should I continue my studies and seek a doctoral degree in Reformation history? It happened that Dr. Meredith Kline was walking by at the time and heard my question. I don't think he stopped walking. He just looked over, smiled, and said, "You can't."

His comment surprised me and led me to think carefully about what he meant. Over the years I have often thought that his remark was some of the best advice I ever got. Dr. Kline was certainly not saying that we cannot know anything about God's will. He had taught us with passion that the Bible is God's revelation and that everything in it is true and an expression of the will of God. Wherever the Bible speaks, we know the will of God.

Dr. Kline did mean that since the Bible does not say specifically whether Bob Godfrey should enter the ministry or study Reformation history, Bob Godfrey cannot with certainty know the will of God on that question. God will not whisper in our ears or write advice on notepaper for us. God does not want us to pursue a mystic experience for direction in life. Rather, he wants us to take responsibility as creatures made in his image to choose a wise course of action.

Again, Dr. Kline was not saying that God is uninterested or uninvolved in our decisions as his children. He gives us his Word, which tells us many things that ought to inform our choices. He gives us his Spirit, who renews our minds and wills so that we seek to please him. He gives us the church and the Christian community so that we can be helped by the insights and wisdom of others. He orders our lives in his providence so that we have certain interests and abilities as well as certain opportunities. He gives us the privilege of coming to him in prayer with all our concerns and needs. But he leaves us to weigh our gifts and opportunities, and then to choose a path that we think will be pleasing to him.

We may find after we have walked a certain path for a while that we ought to do something else. Does that mean that the original choice was wrong? Not necessarily. It may mean that God now wants us to do something else. Sometimes we can see the full significance of a decision only long after we make it.

In that third year of seminary, I made several choices. I decided that if I were to study Reformation history, I wanted to do that back at Stanford. So I applied only to Stanford. I thought that if I were not admitted, then clearly I should pursue ordination. But I also knew that I could not simply assume that if I were admitted to Stanford, that would be a clear sign that God wanted me to go there. Not every opportunity that opens before us is one that we ought to take.

When I was accepted at Stanford, I still had to ponder whether I ought to go there. I finally concluded that I should, for a variety of reasons. I believed that I had the ability to do that study and that my earlier education had equipped me well to be successful in it. I knew languages that were important to the study: Latin, German, French, and Dutch. I loved studying that period in history. I hoped that I could use that education to teach in a seminary and to help the church through that teaching. I also remembered hearing Dr. Spitz reflect on the time he had had to make the same decision. He too had gone to seminary and had had to choose between the pastoral ministry and further study. He said that he finally realized that he liked books more than people. I think in 1970 I felt drawn toward study in the same way.

As I studied sixteenth-century history, I began to understand more fully the Reformation idea of calling. The Reformers created a revolution for Christians with their new (and biblical) teaching on calling. In the Middle Ages, the church had come to teach that only priests, monks, and nuns had a call (in Latin, *vocatio*) from God. Everyone else lived in this world without a divine calling for life and work. The Reformers rejected the idea that only clerics and ascetics were called by God. They insisted that all the lives of Christians faithfully lived before God were callings. Martin Luther was especially eloquent on this point, in his typically ironic way: "All callings are honorable before God, with the possible exceptions of burglary and prostitution."

The Reformers had come to see that the farmer or shopkeeper was as truly a servant of God in his work as was the minister in his. They saw that the loving husband and wife and

85

the faithful parents were serving God as much as the unmarried missionary. They reached this conclusion from their careful study of the Word of God. They acknowledged that 1 Corinthians 7:32–38 teaches that it is better for some people in certain kinds of work to be unmarried in their service to God. Certain kinds of missionary work, for example, may require such time and commitments that marriage would be impossible. But Luther said that this was not because the unmarried state was inherently more holy than the married state. He wrote, "It is God's word and preaching which make celibacy—such as that of Christ and Paul—better than the estate of marriage. In itself, however, the celibate life is far inferior." He insisted, "The dearest life is to live with a godly, willing, obedient wife in peace and unity."

Luther and the other Reformers derived their understanding of calling in part from what they found in Genesis 1 and 2. There they clearly saw God's original intention for mankind before the fall into sin. Marriage—far from being only a remedy for lust, as many medieval Christians thought— was good and was a proper part of the life of the holy ones of God. Marriage and other elements of Christian calling were truly "creation ordinances" and part of a "creation mandate"— as the Reformed would later call them.

God made it clear in the creation account what mankind's original calling or purpose was. Only men and women in all creation would bear the image of God. Even the angels were not given that honor. To bear the image of God certainly means that we humans are creatures with immortal souls who are to live in holiness before God. It also means that as image-bearers, men and women at creation were entrusted with several responsibilities. Although sin has in many ways distorted and deformed these responsibilities and their fulfillment, they remain the ideal toward which we must press.

The first responsibility is to work. Work is not a result of the fall into sin, but it is part of the nobility of human life in service to God. "Then God said, 'Let us make man in our image, in our likeness, and let them rule over the fish of the sea and the birds of the air, over the livestock, over all the earth, and over all the creatures that move along the ground' " (Gen. 1:26). All the earth and everything in it is given to man for his care and keeping. This is part of the "glory and honor" with which man is crowned by God (Ps. 8:5). This means that all work done in God's world to honor God is a calling from him.

This Reformation understanding of work means that the medieval division of the world into sacred and secular realms is rejected. All work is sacred. The six days of work each week are as much with God and for God as the one day of rest. There are no second-class citizens in the kingdom of God. The mother serves God as truly as the minister.

The effect of the Reformation idea of calling was that every Christian has a responsibility to think carefully about how his faith controls his work. All work must be done with honesty and with an eager desire to rule and subdue that part of creation to honor God. We are not Christians only at church or at prayer, but everywhere we are and in all that we do.

The second responsibility given to mankind at creation was to establish families. "God blessed them and said to them, 'Be fruitful and increase in number; fill the earth and subdue it' " (Gen. 1:28). When Adam was first created, he was alone— which was not good (Gen. 2:18). So God created Eve as a "suitable helper" (Gen. 2:20). Also, in Genesis 2:24 we read, "For this reason a man will leave his father and mother and be united to his wife, and they will become one flesh." Here is the foundation of marriage: loving union and help between man and wife and the bearing of children to fill the earth.

The God who existed in the eternal fellowship of three persons established the family as the primary fellowship for his image-bearers. God established the marriage relationship for physical, emotional, and spiritual support for humans. He also gave children as a further blessing. Luther spoke eloquently of the primary duty of parents to children: "Now since we are all duty bound to suffer death, if need be, that we might bring a single soul to God, you can see how rich the estate of marriage is in good works. God has entrusted to its bosom souls begotten of its own body, on whom it can lavish all manner of Christian works. Most certainly father and mother are apostles, bishops, and priests to their children, for it is they who make them acquainted with the gospel."

The third responsibility given at creation was to worship. "God blessed the seventh day and made it holy, because on it he rested from all the work of creating that he had done" (Gen. 2:2–3). God rested not because he was tired but because he wanted to show his image-bearers that they too must rest on the Sabbath day. So he blessed the Sabbath and made it holy, not because he needed a holy day, but because we need one. We need a day to pause from our ordinary labors, to rest and to focus on God.

The Sabbath was not given just to Israel in the days of Moses. It was a need of mankind even before the fall into sin. As finite creatures, we can focus on only one or two things at once. If we are thinking of work or family, we cannot always be thinking of God. So God instituted time to be spent with him. The Sabbath is time for the focused fellowship with God that we have in worship. Since man's fall into sin, our need for worship and time with God has been greater than ever. He has set aside one day in seven (not one hour in a week) for focusing on him. We must not attempt to be wiser than God in thinking that we can flourish with less time with him.

My sense of calling relates to all three of these creation ordinances. For my work I chose the study and teaching of Reformation history because, as I evaluated myself and the situation in which God had placed me, I believed that that was how I could best serve God. Through the years I have expanded that original sense of calling by teaching other periods of church history than just the Reformation, and I have given time to the administrative life of the seminary. But my greatest interest has continued to be in the theology and work of the Reformers. Over the years I have continued to grow in my appreciation of John Calvin. Luther is more quotable, but Calvin is the careful, balanced theologian and pastor. Calvin is still the best of the Reformed theologians. To be sure, other theologians have surpassed him on particular points in the study of the Bible or theology. But when it comes to a comprehensive presentation and appreciation of the Scriptures' message as a whole, Calvin is supreme. The clarity of Calvin's exposition of the Bible, the fullness of his understanding of the work of Christ and of the gospel, his stress on the importance of the church and its ministry, and his appreciation of the certainty of God's mercy for his own are all unrivaled.

My calling to marriage began in the back seat of a car on the way to church one Sunday morning. Rob Johnston had offered to take me to church my freshman year at Stanford. A friend of Rob's sister, a very attractive brunette whom I had not met before, was also in the car. She was introduced to me as Mary Ellen Nemeth. She was much older than I—a sophomore. She does not actually remember this meeting, but I do. She had a very well-turned ankle—as the Victorians used to say.

Although we saw each other from time to time at church and at InterVarsity meetings on campus, we did not actually begin to keep company until her senior year. She too was a history major, a student of American and modern European history. She had been born and raised in Cleveland, Ohio. All of her grandparents had been born in Hungary, and Hungarian was her first language. She had been raised in a Hungarian Baptist church, but I remembered that Calvin had led his wife-to-be out of the Anabaptist church. After she graduated, she returned to Cleveland to study history and get a teaching credential, which proved invaluable as the financial foundation for my future studies. (But I did not marry her for her credential!)

We were married in June 1968 after a courtship of nearly three years. We have now been married nearly 35 years, and Mary Ellen has been a perfect helpmeet. She has been an ideal partner in every way, providing a wonderful home, encouraging my work, and using her remarkable talents as a teacher of history to help many generations of high school students. I have experienced Luther's sentiments: "No sweeter thing than love of woman—may a man be so fortunate."

Mary Ellen and I have been blessed with three children: William, Mari, and Robert. Raising children has brought surprises into our lives. I was surprised how interesting my children were compared to the children of my friends. I was surprised that my friends preferred to talk about their children rather than listen to stories about mine. I continue to be surprised at how three children born of the same parents and raised in the same household can be so different. I am profoundly thankful to God that all three have professed their faith in Christ and are communicant members in our church. They are each pursuing quite diverse careers: William a lawyer, Mari a teacher, and Robert still in college, but very interested in music and improvisational theater. My children have taught me much about life and about myself—especially about laughter and patience (or the need for it). Family life, as Roland Bainton summarized Luther's view, is truly "the school of character."

In addition to my callings as historian and husband and father, I was also called to the ministry of the Word and sacraments. My first full-time job as a church historian began in 1974 at Westminster Theological Seminary in Philadelphia. We joined the Christian Reformed Church in Broomall, Pennsylvania. In addition to my seminary teaching, I taught adult Sunday school (something I have continued ever since), served as an elder, and exhorted in churches that needed someone to lead their services. After some time, several Christian Reformed ministers and Dr. Edmund Clowney, president of the seminary, urged me to pursue ordination. I was uncertain what to do. I felt committed to the Christian Reformed Church, but I knew that ordinarily one had to attend Calvin Theological Seminary in Grand Rapids, Michigan for at least one year in order to be ordained. Through the good offices of Dr. John Kromminga, president of Calvin Seminary, the synod of the CRC waived that requirement, and I was ordained in 1979.

The call to the ministry has given me the great privilege of leading the people of God in the worship of God on the Lord's Day. As a result, some Sundays have not been days of physical rest for me. But they have certainly been days of sharing in the spiritual rest provided in Jesus Christ. From the beginning, I have had a profound sense of the importance of preaching and the sacraments as means of grace. They are the institutions appointed by God in which we as his people should especially look for grace and growth in believing.

Perhaps it is strange that in my continuing shyness I found preaching and teaching relatively easy. And in so doing, I have overcome that shyness. (Actually, Mary Ellen claims credit for my current extroverted state.) In those early years of ministry, I found the pastoral side of the ministry more difficult. But several terms as elder and a variety of pastoral experiences over the years have helped me see both the joys and the importance of that side of the ministry.

My various callings have brought me a great deal of joy and a great sense of fulfillment. When I was a third-year seminarian, I had no idea what God's will was for my future. Looking back, I can see a pattern and coherence that was not apparent at the time various decisions had to be made. But in each major decision I believed that God was calling me to an area of service, and at each step he has confirmed and encouraged my choices.

The Reformed doctrine of calling does not tell us that we can know God's will for our future before we make any decisions. But it does assure us that as we make decisions, God is indeed with us and does have a sovereign plan that he will fulfill in our lives. It is also comforting in times of difficulty, when we may question our way in life, to know that God has called us to fulfill the responsibilities given to us. He has called us, and he will give us what we need for our callings.

History

PSALM   7 8 : 1 - 8 ,   6 5 - 7 2

My conversion redirected my early interest in history toward the history of the Reformation. The great Reformation of the sixteenth century is a fascinating period of history by any standard. It abounds with individuals—some famous and some not—who were influential, courageous, and heroic. It is a time in which some fundamental changes were taking place in Europe—changes that moved the Western world out of the medieval era and into the modern world. Developments that we take for granted—ranging from the nation state, to democracy, capitalism, general education, modern natural science—were all initiated or speeded in their development by the events of the sixteenth century.

While the entire period of the Reformation interested me, I knew that in my doctoral work I would have to choose a very specific topic on which to write my dissertation. My principal adviser, Dr. Spitz, was primarily interested in the relationship of Renaissance learning to the rise of Lutheranism. But he very generously encouraged my interest in Calvin and Calvinism. At that time, the study of some aspect of Calvin's life or thought seemed too big an undertaking for me. Because of my connection with the Dutch Reformed tradition and because of Dr. Nicole's help in learning Dutch, I thought that some topic relating to the growth of Calvinism in the Netherlands would be good for me. Since I had already studied the theology of the Canons of the Synod of Dort with Dr. Nicole, I began to think that a study of the historical context of the synod (which had met in the Dutch city of Dordrecht from November 1618 to May 1619) would be valuable.

As a historical researcher, I have always felt remarkably like a detective. I first must learn what other historians have already discovered so that I do not repeat their work. Then I must clarify exactly what I want to try to discover. Next I must begin hunting for evidence, never quite sure that the evidence I need actually exists. Finally, I must take whatever evidence I can find and analyze it to see what it teaches about the past, revise any theories that I had developed in light of this evidence, and then reach a conclusion.

My detection on the Synod of Dort convinced me that much could still be written about the historical background to the doctrinal conclusions or Canons of Dort that would illumine those discussions. In the summer of 1972, Mary Ellen and I traveled to Europe so that I could do some research for my dissertation. It was a wonderful summer, even if Mary Ellen did observe that I had taken her on the library tour of Europe. I spent days in the Reading Room of the British Museum gathering materials on the British delegation to Dort. We visited libraries in Oxford and Cambridge and then did research in the Old Synodical Archive in The Hague. It was a treat to see the actual handwritten minutes of the synod. We also traveled to Geneva to investigate materials on the Genevan delegates to Dort. It was great fun.

For me, however, history is always more than simply fun. I have always sensed that history is immensely useful. History is a mirror that helps us to see ourselves more clearly. It shows us where we have come from and often reveals why we do things. (A little case in point—in many churches of the Dutch Reformed tradition, the elders and deacons meet with the minister to pray before the service. Where does this practice come from? It is, of course, a useful exercise of piety, but it is not required in the Bible. Apparently the practice developed in the 1830s when some Dutch churches had seceded from the state Reformed church. The services of these churches were sometimes attacked by mobs, and the elders developed the practice of meeting with the minister to establish an escape route if things became too dangerous.)

The Bible shows us in many ways the importance and usefulness of history. The Old Testament contains a great deal of history, not only in the Pentateuch and the books of Samuel, the Kings, and the Chronicles, but also in the prophets. Creation, fall, and redemption all occur in history. God works in and through history to accomplish his purposes. History is also important in the New Testament. More than half of it is composed of the Gospels and Acts, which are primarily history.

Psalm 78, one of the historical psalms, points us to the importance of history for the people of God. The first point made in this psalm is that history is wisdom. It informs and enlightens the child of God seeking to live for God. "I will open my mouth in parables" (Ps. 78:2) reminds us of the language of the book of Proverbs. The Hebrew word translated *parables* here is translated as *proverbs* in Proverbs 1:1–6: "The proverbs of Solomon son of David, king of Israel: for attaining wisdom and discipline; for understanding words of insight; for acquiring a disciplined and prudent life, doing what is right and just and fair; for giving prudence to the simple, knowledge and discretion to the young—let the wise listen and add to their learning, and let the discerning get guidance—for understanding proverbs and parables, the sayings and riddles of the wise." A proverb is a distillation of wisdom gained from some experience or insight. In Psalm 78 the wisdom is drawn from the history of God's people in the first years after they had left Egypt.

The wisdom found in history, however, is not always self-evident or easy to see. History often seems rather to be "things hidden from of old" (Ps. 78:2). Someone must explain the true meaning of history. God establishes the meaning of biblical history by inspiring the human authors. The truth that we are to gain from it is therefore certain. Biblical history is like no other. Many events that would be important to secular history are not even mentioned as the inspired authors show us what we must know in the history of redemption, while they magnify many apparently small events important in God's view. For example, Roman historians did not notice the death of Jesus, but the Bible shows us that it was the turning point of human history.

The insight that God has given into the meaning of the history of his people must be cherished and taught from generation to generation. As generations pass, many events of nations and families and individuals are simply lost and become irretrievable. But some of history, God tells us, must be remembered to help us live as the people of God. Psalm 78 solemnly reminds the people of God of the duty to keep the "family history" alive by passing it on carefully from generation to generation. If we look closely at Psalm 78:5–6, it seems that five generations are mentioned. From a human perspective, that is a long time. How many of us know much about our great-great-grandparents? But God charges us to keep the history of redemption before our eyes and to teach the rising generations about our truest history.

The wisdom that we should gain from a study of the history of the people of God in general, and the history in Psalm 78 in particular, is summarized in verse 7: "Then they would put their trust in God and would not forget his deeds but would keep his commands." We see three benefits to the study of history here: we learn to trust, to remember, and to obey. These virtues may seem to be obvious and clear in the lives of God's people. But history teaches us that they often seem not to characterize Christian living. As verse 8 puts it, "They would not be like their forefathers—a stubborn and rebellious generation, whose hearts were not loyal to God, whose spirits were not faithful to him." These sins of the fathers seem to be set in contrast to the virtues that should mark Christians. Too often the fathers were not obedient, but stubborn and rebellious. Too often they did not remember God's mercy to them and provision for them, but were disloyal to him. Too often they were not trusting, but became faithless.

The wisdom we should gain is first to compare ourselves to history and see how much we take after our fathers. Have we learned the dangers and patterns of sin that surround and tempt us? Are we more characterized by faith, remembrance, and obedience or by unbelief, forgetfulness, and disobedience? We often want to think that we face completely new problems and circumstances and thus to excuse our sin. But when we study the history of God's people, we are reminded, "No temptation has seized you except what is common to man" (1 Cor. 10:13).

Second, this history should teach us that we cannot achieve a stable relationship with God by our hard work. We should work hard at living for our God, but we must see that whatever progress in holiness that we attain really comes from God and from his work. The end of Psalm 78 shows us that hope and healing comes only from God. The solution to our struggles is that God awakes to save (v. 65). He fights for us against all our enemies (v. 66). And his sovereign choice and good pleasure are the foundation of all our blessings. He chose Judah to be the leading tribe and chose Zion to be his capital (v. 68). He did not choose Joseph or his son—which from a human perspective would have been the logical choice in light of Joseph's earlier leadership in saving the people in Egypt (v. 67). He chose David to be king, even though among the sons of Judah David seemed an unlikely choice (vv. 70–71). At every point God reminds us that his sovereign choice determines history and works out salvation for his people.

David is presented as the great savior of his people in Psalm 78. He is the shepherd "with integrity of heart" and "with skillful hands" (v. 72). Yet history tells us that while David was a man after God's own heart, he was far from being a perfectly good shepherd. Only great David's greater Son, Jesus, perfectly fulfilled the role symbolized in David.

In a sense, the history of the church from the time of the apostles continues to serve us as a source of wisdom. We do not have, of course, an inspired interpretation of that history. The meaning of church history therefore cannot be known with certainty. But it still has real usefulness for the people of God. It can serve as a warning, especially of the ways in which the church in various ages accommodated to the cultures in which it found itself. Church history can serve as an inspiration as we consider the heroic ways in which some Christians have lived out their faith. It is also a treasure that preserves the insights into the truth that other ages and times have achieved.

If we live only in the present, we will not really know who we are, and we will deprive ourselves of some of the profound wisdom of the past.

An interest in history, of course, also has its dangers. We can romanticize the past so that we think everything in the past was much better than it is today. We can gloss over the sins and faults of heroes of the past and exaggerate their goodness or significance. We can become so nostalgic about the past that we refuse to live in our own time and face our unique problems and responsibilities. We can fall into the folly that Ecclesiastes warns us about: "Do not say, 'Why were the old days better than these?' For it is not wise to ask such questions" (Eccl. 7:10).

My study of the Synod of Dort was not merely an exercise in nostalgia. My study of Dort yielded important biblical and pastoral insight as I focused on the historical background to the second head of doctrine in the Canons. (Dissertations are about knowing more and more about less and less!) The second head of doctrine dealt with this question: For whom did Christ die? The Arminians insisted that Christ had died for all the sins of every human. The Calvinists rejected this idea and taught that Christ had died only for all the sins of the elect.

At Dort the Calvinists from all over Europe were agreed that Christ had died for the elect. They argued that the Bible said that Christ had given his life a ransom for many (Matt. 20:28) and that Bible verses that seemed to teach a universal atonement had been misunderstood. They maintained that the Arminian doctrine must lead to the conclusion that all are saved: if Christ died for all the sins of all men, then all must be saved. They also insisted that the Arminian teaching creates a contradiction in the Trinity: the Father intends to save the elect alone and the Holy Spirit gives the gift of faith only to the elect, but the Son dies with the intention to save all. All the Calvinists at Dort agreed that the Bible and sound theology taught that Christ had died only for the elect.

Some of the delegates to Dort, however, worried about the adverse reaction to this teaching among non-Calvinists. They feared that it would make Calvinism more difficult to accept and unnecessarily offend some people. These delegates came especially from Germany and Great Britain where many people were not Calvinists. The concerns of these delegates— after some very serious debate and even one challenge to a duel on the floor of the synod—were incorporated into the Canons of Dort. We see these conclusions at two points in particular.

First, the Canons declare that the death of Christ is sufficient to save the whole world. "The death of the Son of God is the only and most perfect sacrifice and satisfaction for sin, and is of infinite worth and value, abundantly sufficient to expiate the sins of the whole world" (Canons II, 3). Dort did not want to suggest any insufficiency or limit to the value of the death of Christ. As many Reformed theologians would say over the years, the death of Christ was sufficient to save the whole world and a thousand worlds besides. Because Jesus was both the Son of God and the perfectly obedient man, his death was of infinite value and merit in the sight of his Father.

Second, some delegates were very concerned to make it clear that their teaching of a definite or limited atonement did not imply that the gospel ought not to be preached to everyone or that anyone coming in faith to Christ would not be received and saved. "Moreover, the promise of the gospel is that whosoever believes in Christ crucified shall not perish, but have eternal life. This promise, together with the command to repent and believe, ought to be declared and published to all nations, and to all persons promiscuously and without distinction, to whom God out of His good pleasure sends the gospel" (Canons II, 5). The gospel must be proclaimed and all called to faith and repentance. Those who do not believe cannot blame Christ for their destruction. "And, whereas many who are called by the gospel do not repent or believe in Christ, but perish in unbelief, this is not owing to any defect or insufficiency in the sacrifice offered by Christ on the cross, but is wholly to be imputed to themselves" (Canons II, 6).

As I have continued to reflect on this Calvinist doctrine over the years, I have become more convinced that it is biblical. Jesus did indeed lay down his life for his sheep (John 10:15). I have also seen the pastoral wisdom of the teaching. When I was an undergraduate, I observed a well-meaning Arminian witness to an unbelieving friend. He said, "God loves you, and Christ died for you." The unbeliever responded, "Well, then, I am safe as I am. If God loves me and Christ died to save me, I cannot be in any danger." What we need to say to unbelievers is this: "Christ died to save sinners. If you come to him in true faith, you will find in his work on the cross a complete payment for all your sins." Even my narrowly focused doctoral studies have been useful to me.

My broader study of Calvinism has led me to appreciate its profound impact on the formation of modern Western society. Historians—both Christians and non-Christians—recognize the vital contribution made to the modern world by the Reformed movement. Calvinism, which today often seems very small and marginalized, has made a great impact on the world around us.

Look at education. Scotland was the first country in Europe to attain universal literacy. Why was that? Because Calvinists there believed so strongly that all people needed to be able to read the Bible for themselves. Schools grew not just to make good citizens (although that was certainly an important factor for Calvinists), but especially to make good Christians. Education of boys and girls was a critical factor in the development of Western civilization.

Look at economics. John Calvin was the first Christian theologian to teach that charging interest on a loan was not sinful. He and his followers also taught the virtue of not spending all that one earns, but saving and investing something of what one earns. Here are critical ideas and disciplines foundational to modern capitalist economies.

Look at the rise of modern natural science. Many leading early scientists were Calvinists. Reformed Christianity believed that the only way to understand the world was by studying it directly. They saw science as an honorable calling through which the ways of our God as the great Creator could be learned. They rejected the idea that nature was too holy or too unimportant to study. They appreciated the value of the world that their God had made.

Finally, look at the political impact of Calvinism. Calvin himself was a rather medieval man on several important political issues. He did not believe that democracy was the best form of government, and he did not believe in religious freedom. He did believe, however, that Christians as citizens had a responsibility to promote justice. He believed that if a government had become tyrannical, responsible citizens had a right and duty to rebel against that tyranny in the name of justice. This Calvinistic conviction led to changes of government in the Netherlands, in Scotland, in England, and in the American colonies. When such changes in government occurred, often a movement toward limited, representational government followed. The virtues of Calvinism shaped the sense of duty for citizens in many modern democracies.

History is fun—or should be. Dr. Spitz used to say that history is so inherently interesting that one has to work very hard to make it dull. He would then add that many historians are very hardworking. History is useful. We learn in significant ways who we are by knowing where we come from. And history can be inspirational as we reflect on heroes great and small who shaped the past for us.

The great glory of Calvinism, however, is not its cultural power or influence. The greatest historical significance of Calvinism is its passion to be faithful to the Scriptures in its doctrine, its church organization, its worship, and its piety. The most valuable legacy of Calvinism to us is its biblical fidelity.

Dual Citizenship

E P H E S I A N S   2

By California standards, the roots of my family are deep in this state. My great-great-grandfather Godfrey came to California in the 1880s. Henry and Martha Godfrey were English, came to America in about the 1860s, settled for a time on the East Coast, and then moved to California. They are buried in the hills of the eastern Bay Area in northern California. Other ancestors also came rather early to California. My mother's family, the Manters, came to America from England in probably the eighteenth century, and were also in California by the late nineteenth century. My maternal grandmother, Annie Collins, and her family lived north of the Bay Area in and around Sebastopol. My paternal grandmother's father, a Rogers, helped fight the great San Francisco fire in 1906. In different parts of the family we counted farmers and loggers, carpenters and craftsmen, and more recently insurance people.

In many places today it is common to speak disparagingly of California. I can understand that. California is crowded in some regions; it seems symbolized by freeways and Hollywood. California for some epitomizes all that seems opposed to Christian faith and life. But for me California is a place of great beauty and variety, with its cities and vineyards, its wild coast and fine beaches, its valleys and mountains. I feel at home here.

My family were all proud Americans. My father served in the army for five years during World War II. He and my grandfather were mayors of our hometown. My grandfather helped weed out local political corruption and was rewarded with a park named after him. One of my treasured possessions is a picture taken at the dedication of that park in 1946. I was there as a babe in arms with my father, grandfather, and great-grandfather.

My upbringing was almost entirely in northern California. Once we spent an afternoon in Tijuana, and a few times we went to the Nevada side of Lake Tahoe. I think in my first twenty years I went only once to southern California. (In those days, northern Californians had a vast sense of superiority over southern Californians.) My life was happy and secure and lived within rather narrow borders.

After my first year in college I had an opportunity to study overseas, and my parents encouraged me to do that. They very generously provided for nine months in Europe. I traveled on brief trips to Prague, Switzerland, and Paris. A three-week trip took me with friends to Mt. Athos to visit very old Greek Orthodox monasteries as well as Athens, Venice, Rome, and Florence. I was able to see some of the remarkable places of Western history. But most of those nine months was spent in a small German village. It was a remarkable time to learn a new language and a new culture and to make friends with people very different from myself.

As I look back on that time from June 1964 to March 1965, I have a very different perspective from what I thought at the time. It was my first occasion to be away from home for any length of time. Being in a new place and culture, away from my family, my homeland, and my church, helped me think in a new way about what it meant to be an American and a Christian. I began to face new issues of citizenship.

At age 19 in 1964 I went to Germany with a sense that World War II was an event in the rather distant past. I never considered that I might meet any anti-American feeling because of the war. And, as far as I noticed, I never did. The Cold War seemed the more pressing reality at the time. West Germans generally seemed very grateful for the help they received from America.

When we visited Berlin, we saw the wall that had been erected only about two years before. We saw the visible evidence of the Iron Curtain dividing east from west. After seeing many of the sights of West Berlin, several times we crossed through Checkpoint Charlie to visit East Berlin. I attended services in a large downtown church there. The congregation was rather small and old, but I was impressed with the sermon. The preacher asked how Christians ought to live under a Communist government. He said that they were to avoid two extremes: they were not to become resigned and hopeless, nor were they to become revolutionaries hoping to change the government by their own actions. Rather, they were to live in a confident hope that God would preserve and provide for them.

When we passed through Checkpoint Charlie, we walked across a rather barren open area before passing through another wall into East Berlin. That open area contained the place where

Hitler's Chancellery had stood and where the bunker in which Hitler had died was buried. The bombed-out shells of buildings near the wall in East Berlin were a clear reminder that in fact the Second World War was not so far in the past.

I was in Germany primarily as a student. Stanford had a campus in a rural setting where we could study German and other courses in English, so that we could have the experience of living in another country without delaying the progress of our education. This campus was in the countryside outside of Stuttgart. Several little villages were nearby, and a number of the townspeople regularly made students welcome in their homes whenever they could visit.

In the village of Endersbach I got to know a German family who were exceedingly friendly and hospitable. They attended a small Baptist church there in the village, and I attended with them. Frieder and Gisela Diemer had two young sons and for several years had entertained American students from the Stanford campus just up the hill. They were patient with several of us who visited as our German slowly—very slowly—improved. They helped us to learn the local dialect, Schwaebish. They took us out to the small plots of land on which they grew various fruits and vegetables. They showed us the apple juice and sauerkraut that they made every year. They shared delicious food and holiday celebrations with us. I especially remember Christmas in their home. I remember sitting around the Christmas tree reading the Christmas story from Luke's gospel and praying together. (I kept my eyes open during the prayer because the real candles on the tree made me very nervous.)

Through the Diemers I got to know Gisela's father, Herr Schwegler, and over time learned something of his story. He was a faithful member of the Baptist congregation. Before the war his family had experienced some harassment because many Germans believed that the Baptist church was a cult. Only after the war did Baptists become more respectable because so many American soldiers were Baptists. During the war the harassment increased—especially from one Nazi family—because Herr Schwegler insisted that his children attend church instead of the Hitler Youth meetings on Sundays. After the war, when the Allies occupied the village, the Allies took over the house where that strong Nazi family with a number of young children lived—leaving them homeless. Others in the village were afraid to take them in for fear of appearing to be pro-Nazi. But the Schweglers took the other family into their home, believing that they should live out their Christianity by loving their enemies even if it placed them in some danger. The Schweglers later learned that their names, along with the names of all the other strong Baptists, were listed in the city hall as people to be eliminated after Hitler won the war. Here were people who lived their faith.

Today we would say that I had had a wonderful cross-cultural experience in Germany. I came to appreciate a different culture and a different language through the lives of several remarkable people. But more importantly, I had come to see the ways in which Christianity united different people even across those cultural lines.

We as Christians have a deeper allegiance than to any of the nations of this world. However much we love the countries in which we were born or to which we have immigrated, our ultimate loyalty must be to the kingdom that Christ is inaugurating. Paul reminded the Philippians of that truth. The Philippians were very proud of their status as a Roman colony and therefore as Roman citizens. To them Paul wrote that "our citizenship is in heaven" (Phil. 3:20). Paul urged them to take him as their example: "Forgetting what is behind and straining toward what is ahead, I press on toward the goal to win the prize for which God has called me heavenward in Christ Jesus" (Phil. 3:13–14).

This perspective of the apostle Paul ought to challenge a common proverb, "Blood is thicker than water." This proverb has the general meaning that family ties will usually prevail over other loyalties. What was the original meaning of the water in the expression? It probably referred to the water of baptism. The proverb, then, is a warning that although the water of baptism is supposed to create a new family and new sense of identity, when push comes to shove, family will be more important than baptism. This proverb is no doubt often true in human experience, but it ought not to be so among genuine Christians. Our connection to Christ is our deepest responsibility, and we ought to confess with Luther, "Let goods and kindred go, This mortal life also; The body they may kill: God's truth abideth still; His kingdom is forever."

All Christians recognize that this heavenly citizenship ought to claim our loyalty. But those of us who are Reformed Christians see that citizenship and that kingdom in more specific terms. Heavenly citizenship means that we are members of the heavenly Jerusalem. The church in heaven is the true Zion of God, the spiritual Jerusalem that is our mother. Paul showed the vast difference between the earthly and the heavenly Jerusalems when he wrote, "Now Hagar stands for Mount Sinai in Arabia and corresponds to the present city of Jerusalem, because she is in slavery with her children. But the Jerusalem that is above is free, and she is our mother" (Gal. 4:25–26). Hebrews makes the same point: "But you have come to Mount Zion, to the heavenly Jerusalem, the city of the living God. You have come to thousands upon thousands of angels in joyful assembly, to the church of the firstborn, whose names are written in heaven" (Heb. 12:22–23a). What city do we live in? We are already citizens of the heavenly Jerusalem.

This point about Jerusalem is critical for understanding our Christian citizenship. We are citizens not just of the church and of heaven. By being part of the church, we have become citizens of the true, spiritual Israel. Paul taught very plainly that the Gentiles who were once aliens are now citizens of the true Israel, God's true spiritual people:

> Therefore, remember that formerly you who are Gentiles by birth and called "uncircumcised" by those who call themselves "the circumcision" (that done in the body by the hands of men)—remember that at that time you were separate from Christ, excluded from citizenship in Israel and foreigners to the covenants of the promise, without hope and without God in the world. But now in Christ Jesus you who once were far away have been brought near through the blood of Christ.
>
> For he himself is our peace, who has made the two one and has destroyed the barrier, the dividing wall of hostility, by abolishing in his flesh the law with its commandments and regulations. His purpose was to create in himself one new man out of the two, thus making peace. . . .
>
> Consequently, you are no longer foreigners and aliens, but fellow citizens with God's people and members of God's household. . . . In him the whole building is joined together and rises to become a holy temple in the Lord. (Eph. 2:11–15, 19, 21)

Notice Paul's strong language in this passage in Ephesians. The Gentiles were once separated and excluded. He is

111

crystal clear: they were excluded from citizenship in Israel. But now that situation has changed. By the work of Christ, they are now brought near. To what are they brought near? They are brought near to Israel. Indeed, Christ has eliminated the dividing wall. What wall? Christ removed the dividing wall between Gentiles and Jews, making them one—one new man. The result is that the Gentiles are "no longer foreigners and aliens, but fellow citizens with God's people." Of what kingdom are these Gentiles citizens? Clearly, the Gentiles now share in the citizenship that Paul mentioned just a few verses above: "the citizenship in Israel." God is making the Jews and Gentiles together into the temple in which he will dwell. He is indeed rebuilding the temple with these living stones.

The point of view that we find in Ephesians can be found throughout the New Testament. Paul makes the same point when he says that the Gentiles who have become Christians were formerly wild branches, but have now been grafted into the tree of Israel: "If some of the branches have been broken off, and you, though a wild olive shoot, have been grafted in among the others and now share in the nourishing sap from the olive root, do not boast over those branches. If you do, consider this: You do not support the root, but the root supports you" (Rom. 11:17–18). The Gentiles of the church have been joined to the root of Israel and derive their life from that root.

Elsewhere in the New Testament we find the names and blessings of Israel applied to the church. When Paul blessed the Galatian Christians at the end of his letter, he said to them: "Peace and mercy to all who follow this rule, even to the Israel of God" (Gal. 6:16). James addressed scattered Christians as the twelve tribes: "James, a servant of God and of the Lord Jesus Christ, to the twelve tribes scattered among the nations" (James 1:1). Here he is speaking of more than just Jewish Christians because he refers to his readers generally as believers in Jesus and as part of the church (James 2:1; 5:14).

Peter was particularly strong on this point. He knew one of the great promises that God had made to Israel: "Now if you obey me fully and keep my covenant, then out of all nations you will be my treasured possession. Although the whole earth is mine, you will be for me a kingdom of priests and a holy nation" (Ex. 19:5–6a). Peter applied this promise to the church: "But you are a chosen people, a royal priesthood, a holy nation, a people belonging to God, that you may declare the praises of him who called you out of darkness into his wonderful light" (1 Peter 2:9). Peter taught that the fulfillment of the promise made to Israel is found in the church.

By now, some may feel that I have belabored the obvious. But this aspect of New Testament teaching is by no means obvious to all Bible-believing Christians. Many Christians have accepted a teaching that insists that Israel and the church are two entirely separate and distinct peoples of God and that God deals quite differently with each of these peoples. The issue whether the church is the spiritual Israel or is fundamentally different from Israel is not just a matter of understanding biblical prophecy and the future. It relates to how we use the Old Testament and the law of God. Is the idea of a Sabbath only for Israel? Are the Ten Commandments for the church? Are the children of believers in covenant with God in the New as well as the Old Covenant? Are the psalms the spiritual songs of the church or only the songs of Israel?

All of these questions are very important for the Christian understanding of the character of the spiritual kingdom to which we belong. If the church is the spiritual Israel, then the history of Israel in the Old Testament is not "their" history; it is "our" history. We can sing Psalm 83:2–4: "See how your enemies are astir, how your foes rear their heads. With cunning they conspire against your people; they plot against those you cherish. 'Come,' they say, 'let us destroy them as a nation, that the name of Israel be remembered no more.' " When we sing this psalm, we will know that Israel's enemies are our enemies and that the evil one who misled Edom, Moab, and Philistia still misleads those who hate the church.

We can also sing Psalm 72:8–11: "He will rule from sea to sea and from the River to the ends of the earth. The desert tribes will bow before him and his enemies will lick the dust. The kings of Tarshish and of distant shores will bring tribute to him; the kings of Sheba and Seba will present him gifts. All kings will bow down to him and all nations will serve him." This king is not Solomon in the deepest sense. This universal king is Jesus Christ. Kings have worshiped him, and we have seen the fulfillment of this psalm. Here is our spiritual king-dom clearly laid out for us. Jesus who died under the sign "This is the King of the Jews" is our king.

We need to understand our spiritual citizenship because much in our American culture is anti-Christian. Today the dom-inant culture or cultures of America do not recognize the claims of our Christ as king of kings. They mock the exclusive claims of Christ as the only way to God. They disparage the Bible as the true Word of God. They reject the moral values of our reli-gion. They dismiss the church as an irrelevant institution. We are surrounded as the Philippians were by those who "live as enemies of the cross of Christ. Their destiny is destruction, their god is their stomach, and their glory is in their shame. Their mind is on earthly things" (Phil. 3:18–19). We must see our-selves clearly as the Israel of God in the midst of a lawless nation.

When we do this, we are also protected from some of the aberrations of Christianity prevalent in America. Many American Christians see little binding authority to the law of God or to the church as God's saving institution. They have adopted a form of Christianity so individualistic that the very idea of being a spiritual community seems strange to them. They do not understand the unifying character of the covenant that binds Christian to Christian in the forms of church life that God has ordained.

Some American Christians seem to confuse their two kinds of citizenship. They have linked their Christianity with the early Christian history of America in inappropriate ways. They want to inspire contemporary Christians to create a Christian America patterned after a romantic idea of America's past. Now, as Christian citizens of America we want to advance the cause of justice and righteousness in all ways appropriate to American citizens. But we do not want to confuse our two distinct citizenships as Christians. We must avoid the temptation to conform to a civic religion that makes the well-being and unity of America our highest good. We cannot, for example, take part in worship services for the sake of national unity if Jesus Christ is not honored as the only way to God.

Sometimes our hymns can create a similar kind of confusion. Think, for example, of the hymn "We Praise Thee, O God," written in 1857. One verse reads, "We praise Thee, O God, for Thy guiding hand, In leading Thy Church to freedom's fair land; Through sore persecution our fathers here came, Where free and unfettered they worshipped Thy name." Or consider this verse from the 1833 hymn "O God, Beneath Thy Guiding Hand": "O God, beneath Thy guiding hand Our exiled fathers crossed the sea; And when they trod the wintry strand, With prayer and psalm they worshipped Thee." These verses may express the experience of some Christians and some ethnic groups who came to America, but they cannot speak for all Christians in America. These verses really describe the experience of some English Puritans coming to America. But Christians generally should not be forced to identify with this bit of church history. It is far better to identify with the universal history of all God's people as we find it in the psalms.

Paul was proud of his citizenship in the Roman Empire. He pointed out to a Roman soldier that he was from Tarsus, "a citizen of no ordinary city" (Acts 21:39). He was not hesitant to exercise his rights as a Roman citizen in appealing to Caesar for judgment (Acts 25:11). As Christians, we too should appreciate and exercise our citizenship in the nations of this world. But we must never compromise our primary citizenship, which is in heaven. We need to develop an appreciation of many cultures and peoples and never succumb to an unloving nationalism. Even more, we must always remember that our first loyalty must be to Jesus and his kingdom. Water is thicker than blood. California and America are wonderful, but they are not heaven. As Christians, we seek a city whose builder and maker is God (Heb. 11:10).

Law and Spirit

R O M A N S   6 - 7

One of my spiritual struggles in high school as I was coming to faith was a worry that I did not feel very sinful. I knew that the Bible said I was a sinner. I accepted the Reformed doctrine of total depravity. I believed in original sin. As a matter of faith, I confessed that I was a sinner. But I worried that I did not feel particularly sinful. Was that a sign that I had never really repented? Was my faith not really deep or genuine if I did not have a more profound sense of my own sinfulness?

As the years have passed, this worry has receded. Today I have a much more profound sense of my own sinfulness than I did all those years ago. This development may strike some people as strange. Wouldn't it be more logical to feel more sinful at the beginning of the Christian life and more holy as the years go on? Don't we make progress in holiness as we live the Christian life?

In the spirit of this autobiography, I suppose that I ought now to discuss the particular sins against which I struggle. But

I am not going to do that. I believe that we ought to confess particular sins particularly to God. I also believe that discussing specific struggles with specific sins can be helpful to other Christians who may be struggling with the same sins. But more often I think we should keep our very personal struggles to ourselves or seek help from a trusted minister or friend. The modern American desire to be "transparent" is often carried too far. Sin is an ugly thing and should be paraded only when necessary and for very specific purposes.

What I have learned from my study of Reformed theology and from my own experience is that as we mature as Christians, we grow in both a sense of our sinfulness and a sense of progress in holiness. The more we understand about holiness, the more clearly we see how far we have to go. The more we focus on the holiness of God, the more we see how wretched we still are. The better we appreciate the grace of God in Christ, the more we will see that we have grown in holiness by God's grace. The Heidelberg Catechism wonderfully summarizes this truth after its exposition of the Ten Commandments. The catechism asks, Question 114: "But can those who are converted to God keep these commandments perfectly?" It answers: "No; but even the holiest men, while in this life, have only a small beginning of this obedience; yet so that with earnest purpose they begin to live, not only according to some but according to all the commandments of God." We still have a long way to go, but we do desire to keep all of God's law.

For many Christians today, the law is a confusing subject. Some insist that the Ten Commandments ought to hang on public-school walls but have removed them from the churches. They insist that we as Christians are not under law, but under grace. A cursory look at the New Testament seems to support such Christians. We read that the Old Covenant works death, but the New Covenant brings life (2 Cor. 3:7–9); "the letter kills, but the Spirit brings life" (v. 6). In Romans, Paul seems to speak just as strongly: "through the law comes the knowledge of sin" (Rom. 3:20 NASB); "the law brings about wrath" (Rom. 4:15); "you are not under law, but under grace" (Rom. 6:14); "we have been released from the Law . . . so that we serve in newness of the Spirit and not in oldness of the letter" (Rom. 7:6); "for Christ is the end of the law" (Rom. 10:4). What could be clearer than that the law has no continuing purpose for Christians who are led by the Spirit according to the law of love?

We must always, however, consider the whole Bible. We find equally clear statements that seem to teach the opposite of what we find in the verses quoted above. Jesus said, "Do not think that I came to abolish the Law or the Prophets; I did not come to abolish, but to fulfill. For truly I say to you, until heaven and earth pass away, not the smallest letter or stroke shall pass away from the Law, until all is accomplished. Whoever then annuls one of the least of these commandments, and so teaches others, shall be called least in the kingdom of heaven; but whoever keeps and teaches them, he shall be called great in the kingdom of heaven" (Matt. 5:17–19 NASB). Paul tells us, also in Romans, that the law is "holy, righteous and good" and "spiritual" (Rom. 7:12, 14). He also said, "For in my inner being I delight in God's law" (Rom. 7:23). The prophet Jeremiah defined an essential element of the New Covenant as God promising: "I will put my law in their minds and write it on their hearts" (Jer. 31:33).

Over the years I have returned again and again to the question: how can we give full weight to both of these kinds of verses in the Bible? Once again I have found, through studying history, theology, and the Bible, that Reformed Christianity gives the best answers to this question. To understand the proper uses of the law, we must rightly distinguish between justification (how we are reconciled to a holy God) and sanctification (how we individually become more holy).

Most of my development as a Christian and much of my ministry has been in Dutch Reformed churches. But much of my professional teaching has been among many Presbyterians. While I enjoy as often as possible pointing out the vast superiority of things Dutch Reformed to things Presbyterian, I have learned to appreciate and profit from many things Presbyterian. In the Westminster Larger Catechism we find great help in sorting out this question of the law and its function for Christians. To understand the law, we have to understand the different ways in which it relates to justification and to sanctification. We must recognize that it is one thing to be reconciled to God and quite another to be growing in holiness. Question 77 of the Larger Catechism asks, "Wherein do justification and sanctification differ?" The answer is one of the most helpful brief statements to be found anywhere: "Although sanctification be inseparably joined with justification, yet they differ, in that God in justification imputeth the righteousness of Christ; in sanctification his Spirit infuseth grace, and enableth to the exercise thereof; in the former, sin is pardoned; in the other, it is subdued; the one doth equally free all believers from the revenging wrath of God, and that perfectly in this life, that they never fall into condemnation; the other is neither equal in all, nor in this life perfect in any, but growing up to perfection."

This splendid statement deserves careful examination. First, the catechism reminds us that in the Christian, justification and sanctification always live together. No Christian can claim to be justified, yet have no sanctifying grace in his life. James 2 makes that point emphatically. Second, the catechism stresses that justification and sanctification are not the same, but rather must be clearly distinguished. Perhaps we can see that distinction clearly through putting the differences between them side by side:

Justification	Sanctification
1. Righteousness of Christ imputed	1. Spirit infuses grace
2. Sin is pardoned	2. Sin is subdued
3. All sinners equally free of wrath	3. Sin not equally subdued in all
4. All sinners perfectly freed from wrath now	4. No sinner is perfect in this life, though all are growing

Justification is perfect and equal to all believers in this life because it is the pardoning of sin on the basis of the perfect work of Christ credited to the believer. Sanctification is not equal or perfect in this life because the subduing of sin on the basis of the Spirit's working grace into the life of the Christian advances at different rates in different persons.

If we relate this distinction to the law, we can make sense of the various Scripture texts about the law that we looked at above. The law is good and holy because it expresses the holy will of our holy God. The effect of the law on sinners who understand it is to lead them to despair of their own efforts to save themselves. The law also drives them to rest in Christ, who alone can fulfill the law for them. Those who find forgiveness of sin in Christ are completely free of the law as a means of justification. They have died to the law, and it no longer has any power to condemn them. But those who are justified will love the law as an expression of God's will for them. These Christians will study and treasure the law as a

121

guide for them as they seek to subdue sin in their lives and to live in a holy way.

This truth about justification, sanctification, and the law is not the invention of Reformed theology or the product of my imagination. It is the truth taught in the Bible. We can see that most clearly, perhaps, in Paul's discussion of sanctification in Romans 6 and 7. But before we analyze this section of the Bible, we need to recognize that much controversy has surrounded the interpretation of Romans 7.

The basic debate has been whether the one who struggles against sin is the Christian or the non-Christian. Those who argue for the "Christian" interpretation of Romans 7 point to verse 22, "For in my inner being I delight in God's law," and insist that only a Christian could make such a statement. Those who argue for the "non-Christian" interpretation point to verse 14, "I am unspiritual, sold as a slave to sin," and insist that no Christian could make such a statement. John Calvin and most of the Reformed tradition have followed the "Christian" interpretation of this text. As we follow the development of the apostle Paul's thought, we will see the correctness of this "Christian" interpretation.

Paul in most of Romans 3, 4, and 5 has showed how sinners are saved by the work of Christ alone received by faith alone. He begins Romans 6 with a shocking question: "Shall we go on sinning so that grace may increase?" Since Christ has done all the saving work for sinners and all that sinners have to do is believe, has sin become a good thing that will actually increase grace? As Paul turns from a discussion of justification to a discussion of sanctification, he makes it clear that sin is not good. Those of us who are in Christ will certainly live a new life. Indeed, we are no longer slaves to sin because we have died in Christ to that old authority of sin over us (Rom. 6:1–10).

Paul is so strong about the fact that we have died to sin that we might conclude that sin is no longer possible for us. But Paul clearly rejects that idea because he urges Christians not to sin. When he says that "sin shall not be your master" (Rom. 6:14), he is setting a goal that we need to pursue, not indicating that escape from sin is automatic. In fact, he seems to make an important distinction: "Therefore do not let sin reign in your mortal body so that you obey its evil desires. Do not offer the parts of your body to sin, as instruments of wickedness, but rather offer yourselves to God, as those who have been brought from death to life; and offer the parts of your body to him as instruments of righteousness" (vv. 12–13). This sentiment is very similar to that found in Romans 7:22–23: "For in my inner being I delight in God's law; but I see another law at work in the members of my body, waging war against the law of my mind and making me a prisoner of the law of sin at work within my members." Both of these sections distinguish the inner or deepest self from the members of the body as the outer self.

Since as Christians we are truly slaves of God and not slaves of sin, we ought to live that way. Paul therefore reaches this conclusion: "Just as you used to offer the parts of your body in slavery to impurity and to ever-increasing wickedness, so now offer them in slavery to righteousness leading to holiness" (Rom. 6:19). Although we "have been set free from sin" (Rom. 6:22), we must still work for our sanctification to overcome that sin that remains in us (Rom. 6:15–23).

Paul then shows that the new work we do for sanctification is entirely different from the old way of trying to work to earn our justification. We have completely died with Christ to the law as a way of justification, and we have been raised with Christ to a new life in the Spirit (Rom. 7:1–6).

Is the law useless, then? Not at all. The law still teaches us as Christians what sin is, and by its very holiness and goodness the law shows us how helpless and hopeless we are outside of Christ. The law teaches us in all the struggles and frustrations of trying to live a holy life that we are still in many ways unspiritual and slaves to sin. When I compare the holiness of the law and my continuing falling into sin, I realize that I am wretched. I am a double slave: "So then, I myself in my mind am a slave to God's law, but in the sinful nature a slave to the law of sin" (Rom. 7:25b). Here again we see the distinction between my real, inner nature, renewed in Christ, and my old, continuing sinful nature.

Paul goes on to teach us that we must not be discouraged by the struggle against sin in our lives and the difficulties of progress: "There is now no condemnation for those who are in Christ Jesus" (Rom. 8:1). God has saved us in Jesus, and Jesus sends us his Spirit to help us live for him: "You, however, are controlled not by the sinful nature but by the Spirit, if the Spirit of God lives in you" (Rom. 8:9). You are alive even if your body is dead, and one day the Spirit will make that body alive as well (Rom. 8:10–11). In the meantime we often groan, waiting to be released from this body of death: "We ourselves, who have the firstfruits of the Spirit, groan inwardly as we wait eagerly for our adoption as sons, the redemption of our bodies" (Rom. 8:23).

When Paul links sin particularly to the body, the members, or the flesh, is he asserting a conflict between the physical and the spiritual? Does Paul teach that we are pure in our souls and that sin continues to cling to us only in our bodies? To read Paul this way has led to the rise of Christian asceticism that seeks holiness in the severe discipline of the body— the kind that used to be observed in monasteries. But to read

Paul this way is to misread him. Everywhere in Paul's writings the root of sin is said to be in the soul, not the body. Paul mentions the body because it is the most obvious evidence that we still live in a fallen and dying world. The body, which ages, sickens, and dies, clearly shows that we still await the fullness of redemption in a new heaven and a new earth. A future glory is coming. Until then, we must look to Christ and his Spirit for comfort and strength. We must continue the struggle with sin, seeking both a renewal of our minds and an offering of our bodies as living sacrifices (Rom. 12:1–2).

How do we make progress in subduing sin in our lives? As a Reformed Christian, I learned in early days of my spiritual pilgrimage the value of various Christian exercises for spiritual growth. Personal Bible reading and personal prayer are important. Fellowship and study with other Christians can be very helpful. Special meetings can be encouraging. But the more I have studied and grown as a Christian, the more convinced I am that the foundation of Christian growth is the faithful and careful use of the "means of grace."

What are the means of grace? For Reformed Christians, the means of grace are the preaching of the Word and the administration of the sacraments. Preaching and sacraments, like prayer and fellowship, are divine institutions given by our gracious God for our good. But preaching and sacrament differ from prayer and fellowship as the external, objective ministry of the church to us. Prayer and fellowship are subjective and often internal blessings to us. But God has provided more for us in our weakness. He has provided words and signs that come to us from the outside and remind us of his grace and mercy to us in Christ.

Paul appeals to the means of grace as foundational to his discussion of sanctification in Romans 6: "Or don't you know

125

that all of us who were baptized into Christ Jesus were baptized into his death? We were therefore buried with him through baptism into death in order that, just as Christ was raised from the dead through the glory of the Father, we too may live a new life" (vv. 3–4). Some interpreters have suggested that the baptism that Paul refers to here is not water baptism as a sacrament of the church but baptism in the Spirit. They argue that the baptism to which Paul refers guarantees new life. Because water baptism cannot do that, this baptism must be the baptism of the Spirit.

While this interpretation is possible, it does not strike me as the most likely. Paul had already acknowledged the genuineness of the spiritual life of the Romans to whom he wrote: "We died to sin; how can we live in it any longer?" (Rom. 6:2). When he turns to baptism, he is using that external sacrament that they had all received to reinforce the point he was making. Baptism cannot guarantee that we will finally enjoy the new life in Christ, but it points to that new life and teaches us about it. Too often today we undervalue the sacraments in Reformed churches.

God gave us the sacraments to express the promises of Christ in a visible form to reinforce and support the promises that we hear with our ears in sermons. Augustine called the sacraments visible words. The Westminster Confession calls baptism for the one baptized "a sign and seal of the covenant of grace, of his ingrafting into Christ, of regeneration, of remission of sins, and of his giving up unto God, through Jesus Christ, to walk in newness of life." Baptism stands as God's testimony to the saving work of Christ, which washes away our sins. This Reformed view of baptism stands in marked contrast to the view of most evangelicals, who see baptism primarily as our act of obedience to the Lord's command.

Because baptism is God's promise to us, we need to look to our baptism when we are filled with doubt or discouragement because of sin. Calvin called baptism "a shield to repel doubt." When faith is weak, we need to remember that we are baptized as a sure pledge from God that his promises to us stand firm. Baptism has made the promises of Christ immediate and personal for us. It should be a bulwark of our faith.

The struggle against sin is a real one for every Christian. We need to understand the nature of that struggle and the resources that the Lord has given us in it. The struggle is lifelong as well as daily. There is no quick fix. There is no easy ten-step program to holiness. As Americans, we live in a culture that looks for fast, simple solutions to all problems. As Reformed Christians, we must testify that no such solution exists for the process of sanctification. Rather, we must adorn our faith with a serious discipline and continuous work to grow in grace. But that seriousness must not be grim. We pursue holiness not to earn our standing with God, but because we are filled with love and gratitude to God for the standing that is ours in Christ. We pursue holiness sustained at every point with the grace and support that our God gives us in his church and among his people. We pursue holiness with the confidence that on the day that we are with Christ forever, we will be perfectly holy.

Centrality of Worship

HEBREWS 12:18-29

One of my early attractions to Reformed Christianity was the simplicity, seriousness, and Word-centered character of its worship. That early interest in worship has stayed with me throughout my life. I suppose that was inevitable in light of my studies of the Reformation. The Reformation was not just a reform of doctrine, but also a reform of Christian living and worship.

Medieval Christians' experience of Christianity came primarily through worship and acts of piety. The ritual and mystery of the mass were the central focus of Christian life. So for many at the time of the Reformation, changes in worship were more immediately noticeable and made more of an impact on them than changes of doctrine.

Luther began the changes in worship very slowly and gradually. The greatest changes were saying the mass in German rather than in Latin, removing from the mass the language about offering a sacrifice to God, and having only two sacraments instead of seven. Luther regarded most matters of worship as things indifferent, that is, neither necessarily right nor wrong. Therefore, worship could be changed, but did not have to be changed. Only if a matter of worship was clearly contrary to the Word of God did change have to occur. The result of Luther's approach was that many churches continued to look like Roman Catholic churches with images, altars, and ministers in vestments.

John Calvin and the Reformed fathers at the time of the Reformation were more critical of the tradition of worship that had developed in the late ancient and medieval church. They too wanted to remove anything that was forbidden in the Bible. But they went further and taught that only what the Bible positively commanded should be done in worship.

This Reformed view of worship would later be called the regulative principle of worship. This principle declares that the Bible must regulate or rule over our worship and that only what the Bible teaches either by declaration or by example can be done in our worship. The Heidelberg Catechism states this principle clearly in Question and Answer 96: "What does God require in the second commandment? That we in no wise make any image of God, nor worship Him in any other way than He has commanded in His Word."

The Reformed concern about worship arose from a great desire to avoid idolatry. As the early Reformed leaders read the Bible, they saw God's passion for the purity of his worship. They saw how frequently the Bible presented idolatry as a form of spiritual adultery, in which God's people abandoned their pure and exclusive relationship with God for the gods and forms of worship of the nations. They recognized that God in the summary of his law, the Ten Commandments, had devoted the first two commandments to the prohibition of idolatry: the first forbids the worship of false gods, and the second forbids worshiping the true God in a false way.

The second commandment in particular profoundly influenced Reformed thinking about worship. The judgment of God had fallen severely on Israel for worshiping the golden calf, even though they had called it Jehovah. Aaron's sons were destroyed for offering strange fire on the altar of God. Uzziah was cursed with leprosy for usurping the functions of the priests in the temple. God took his worship seriously, and the Reformed concluded that they must as well.

The Reformed seriousness about worship led to much more profound changes in worship than had occurred among the Lutherans. The Reformed rejected the use of altars, images, and religious symbols in the decoration of their churches. They simplified the ceremonies of worship and the attire of ministers. They eliminated all or almost all the holy days of the church year and eliminated musical instruments from use in public worship. Reformed churches came to look very different from medieval churches.

Not all Reformed churches in Europe applied the regulative principle in the same way or were identical in their worship practices. For example, the Dutch Reformed kept a few hymns alongside their metrical psalms and continued to observe Christmas, Good Friday, Easter, Ascension, and Pentecost—not as obligatory holy days, but as important occasions in redemptive history. Scottish Presbyterians, on the other hand, sang only psalms and banished all elements of a liturgical calendar. When the Dutch Reformed reintroduced musical instruments to worship in the seventeenth century, they did not reject the regulative principle, but rather applied it differently to the question of instruments.

131

Some have argued that the Reformed commitment to the regulative principle really reflects the concerns more of the Old Testament than of the New Testament. God was very concerned for the purity of the worship offered in the temple, but now the temple is fulfilled and replaced by Christ. Christian worship is simple and free. Often it is said, "There is no book of Leviticus in the New Testament." But is this proposed contrast between the Old and New Testaments really accurate?

Paul's letter to the Colossians, for example, shows great concern for the perversions of worship that the apostle found in the Christian church there. He solemnly warned them about not trusting their own ideas or even the supposed guidance of angels when it comes to worship. Paul gives us one of the classic verses to prove the regulative principle in Colossians 2:23: "Such regulations indeed have an appearance of wisdom, with their self-imposed worship." Paul is clearly opposed to self-imposed worship.

In the book of Hebrews, we also find important reflection on the character of Christian worship. Hebrews tells us that part of our privilege as Christians is that we are not confined to an earthly temple, but we have access by faith to the very presence of God in the heavenly temple: "Therefore, brothers, since we have confidence to enter the Most Holy Place by the blood of Jesus, by a new and living way opened for us through the curtain, that is, his body, and since we have a great priest over the house of God, let us draw near to God with a sincere heart in full assurance of faith, having our hearts sprinkled to cleanse us from a guilty conscience and having our bodies washed with pure water" (Heb. 10:19–22).

Hebrews 12 presents a vivid picture of our privilege in the New Covenant by contrasting Mount Sinai with Mount Zion. As Christians, we have not come to Mount Sinai to be terrified by the threatenings of the law. Those threats were to drive the people to look for the coming Messiah. But Jesus the Messiah has come, and in him we as his people come now to Mount Zion, to the heavenly Jerusalem. That heavenly city is crowded in the picture of Hebrews: thousands upon thousands of angels are there. With the angels is all the heavenly church of Jesus, now composed of the spirits of righteous men made perfect. In the midst of all these is Jesus himself, who in his saving work is the mediator between God and man. This heavenly assembly to which we have access by faith is a joyful assembly. As we see Jesus, we are not terrified, but rejoice in the blessing that is ours.

Yet, as Hebrews emphasizes over and over again, we must not be presumptuous about the blessings that are described. We must listen carefully to our God as he calls us to the fellowship of that joyful assembly. We must believe his words to us and faithfully seek to live out our faith before him. We must not cling to this world and its values, but we must rather always remember that this world is going to pass away in judgment. Only the unshakable kingdom of God will remain.

How should we respond to such a great salvation won for us by Jesus and to the kingdom that he has inaugurated? First, our lives must be characterized by gratitude: "Let us be thankful" (Heb. 12:28). Gratitude always draws us away from ourselves and turns our eyes to our God, who has given us all the blessings that we possess.

But Hebrews 12:28 presents a second response expected of God's people: "And so worship God acceptably with reverence and awe." Worship is a necessary response to the saving work of Christ, and we are pointedly reminded that that worship must be acceptable. To whom must it be acceptable? Much contemporary discussion seems to assume that worship must be acceptable to the worshiper. But Hebrews is clear that the first concern of our worship must be that it is acceptable to God. God is not pleased by just any worship offered to him. He remains jealous for his worship; it must please him. The only way to know what worship is acceptable to him and pleases him is through studying his Word. He tells us what pleases him.

We may not have a book of Leviticus in the New Testament, but we do have, for example, Acts 2:42: "They devoted themselves to the apostles' teaching and to the fellowship, to the breaking of bread and to prayer." Luke tells us that the early disciples after Pentecost worshiped by listening to apostolic teaching (the origin of the sermon). They also fellowshiped or had a common experience, best seen today in singing the praises of God together. They also had the Lord's Supper together and prayed. Here is the core of worship that pleases God: sermon, song, sacrament, and supplication. We do not need a book of Leviticus because the worship of the New Covenant is so simple. But its simplicity does not mean that God is encouraging self-imposed worship. God is as committed to God-imposed worship as he ever was.

Today much worship stresses the importance of joy. Joy is indeed a proper and necessary aspect of worship. The angels and church do gather in joyful assembly. But Hebrews 12:28 reminds us that worship is also to be filled with reverence and awe. Joy and reverence are not opposites but are necessary complements in true Christian worship. As Psalm 2:11 says, "Rejoice with trembling."

Why is acceptable and reverent worship so important in the New Covenant? Hebrews 12:29 gives us the answer: "For our God is a consuming fire." The answer is a quotation from the Old Testament, specifically from Deuteronomy 4:24. Hebrews is reminding us that God has not changed his character in the transition from the Old to the New Covenant. He was a consuming fire in the old, and he is a consuming fire in the new.

This quotation from Deuteronomy 4 is particularly significant if we look at its context. The chapter begins with a general call to careful obedience of the revealed will of God: "Hear now, O Israel, the decrees and laws I am about to teach you. Follow them so that you may live and may go in and take possession of the land that the LORD, the God of your fathers, is giving you. Do not add to what I command you and do not subtract from it, but keep the commands of the LORD your God that I give you" (Deut. 4:1–2). From the general call to obedience, Moses becomes specific about idolatry: "You saw no form of any kind the day the LORD spoke to you at Horeb out of the fire. Therefore watch yourselves very carefully, so that you do not become corrupt and make for yourselves an idol, an image of any shape, whether formed like a man or a woman, or like any animal on earth or any bird that flies in the air, or like any creature that moves along the ground or any fish in the water below" (vv. 15–18). Here Moses has moved from a call to obey all the laws of God to a particular focus on the second commandment. He then concludes this section of the chapter with a call to faithfulness: "Be careful not to forget the covenant of the LORD your God that he made with you; do not make for yourselves an idol in the form of anything the LORD your God has forbidden. For the LORD your God is a consuming fire, a jealous God" (vv. 23–24).

In quoting Deuteronomy 4:24, Hebrews recalls God's call to faithfulness and seems to use the second commandment just as the Reformed have always done. From the specific prohibition of images Hebrews infers a broader prohibition against any forms of worship according to human invention. God does not want human creativity in worship but human faith and obedience to his revealed will.

One of the great strengths of Reformed worship has been the care with which Reformed churches have reflected on and practiced the worship of God. But that careful worship has been subjected to a variety of pressures since the sixteenth century. Reformed worship in various countries changed gradually. In America those changes have been more obvious than in some parts of Europe because of the influence of revivalism on the American religious scene.

The Arminian revivalism of nineteenth-century America especially stressed the importance of feeling and emotion in religion. Christian commitment must be felt, and feelings may influence the free will to believe. Music became one of the principal ways in which religious emotions were stimulated at revival meetings. The result was the development of a revival hymnody that stood in marked contrast to the Reformed psalms and the classic hymns of Lutheranism, Anglicanism, and Methodism. The nineteenth-century revival hymn was often more simple in text and more emotional in tune than its musical predecessors. From this same revivalism came the impulse to have special music to enhance the worship service.

Many American Presbyterians and the older Dutch Reformed churches (known as the Reformed Church of America) were greatly influenced by these revivalist developments. Psalms were largely or entirely replaced by hymns, and choirs and other forms of special music became widespread.

These gradual changes continued throughout the nineteenth century and well into the twentieth. New waves of Dutch Reformed immigrants in the early twentieth century immediately recognized the prevailing revivalistic spirit of American religion and declared that the dominant American religion was Methodism, referring not to a denomination but to the character of the Arminian revivalism they observed.

After the middle of the twentieth century, changes in worship accelerated greatly. The increased popularity and influence of the Pentecostal and charismatic movement spearheaded the changes. This movement and the worship changes it led were in fact not a brand-new phenomenon, as some have thought. Pentecostalism is simply a more radical form of Arminian revivalism heightening the role of emotion and experience in worship and the Christian life generally.

Today at the beginning of the twenty-first century, Reformed worship is in danger of extinction in North America. Many conservative Reformed denominations have significantly adopted Pentecostal forms of worship, such as praise bands, praise songs, and prolonged periods of singing called a time of praise and worship. Increasingly the role of the minister as the leader of worship has diminished as an ideal of participation is embraced, with several different persons leading song, prayer, testimonies, and special music.

The new aggressiveness and popularity of revivalistic worship stands as a most serious challenge to all of us who are Reformed. It has certainly led me to spend even more time studying worship and studying the Bible to see if our Reformed approach to worship was just a tradition without biblical foundation. That study has convinced me more than ever that Reformed worship is biblical worship. But if we are to preserve that worship, we as Reformed people must come to a much clearer understanding of that worship. In this brief chapter we cannot do more than survey four basic elements of Reformed worship.

First, we must see public worship as essentially the meeting of God with his covenant people. Worship is not primarily evangelism, teaching, or entertainment. It is not primarily a time of human fellowship. It is a time for the congregation as a community to meet with God.

Second, that meeting with God involves a conversation in which God speaks and his people respond. The speaking of God has the priority. Thus, listening becomes one of the critical skills needed by a worshiper. God speaks in the reading of the Bible, in the sermon, and in the sacraments. (Salutation and benediction can be seen as further ministries of the Word.) As Reformed people, we refer to the sermon and the sacraments as means of grace. They are the means that God uses to help his faithful people grow in grace.

The sermon as an explanation and an application of the Scriptures is God speaking to the congregation. The sacraments are visible manifestations of that same Word of gospel promise. For many evangelical Protestants in our time, the sacraments of baptism and the Lord's Supper seem of very little spiritual importance. But Calvin stressed the importance of the sacraments as God's provision for us in our weakness. For example, he reminds us as Reformed Christians that our baptism needs to be a living spiritual reality for us: "But we must realize that at whatever time we are baptized, we are once for all washed and purged for our whole life. Therefore, as often as we fall away, we ought to recall the memory of our baptism and fortify our mind with it, that we may always be sure and confident of the forgiveness of sins. For, though baptism, administered only once, seemed to have passed, it was still not destroyed by subsequent sins. For Christ's purity has been offered us in it; his purity ever flourishes; it is defiled by no spots, but buries and cleanses away all our defilements" (*Institutes,* IV, 15, 3).

The Reformers gave extensive, careful thought to the sacraments. They grasped that the sacraments were appointed as means of grace through which God comes to his people and builds them up in the faith. These treasures had been well preserved in the liturgical forms for the sacraments that the Dutch Reformed churches have inherited from the sixteenth century. But even in those circles, there is too often an impatience that the forms are too doctrinal or are too familiar. What has surprised me over the years is how unfamiliar the doctrine of those forms often seems to those who have heard them read for years. The Reformed confessions, catechisms, and liturgical forms have summarized the rich sacramental thought of the Reformation and the Bible in a very profitable way. Here is a way for history to live for us and to nourish us in the faith.

In the conversation of worship, God speaks and we respond with prayer and song. Our response must come individually from hearts renewed by the Spirit of God. But that response is expressed corporately as we pray or sing in unison. In this conversation there ought to be movement back and forth between God's speaking and our response. For example, God calls us to worship, and we respond with thanks and praise. God declares his law to us, and we respond with confession of sin.

Third, office is important for Reformed worship. Elders supervise the worship and life of the congregation. Deacons care for the physical needs of the congregation. Ministers preach and lead in worship. The minister is not a priest with magical mediatorial powers standing between God and his people. Neither is he just a popular or talented leader. Rather, he is called by God through the congregation and set apart for certain responsibilities. Since we see the need to be careful in our worship, it surely seems appropriate that the one who leads worship should be called, examined, and ordained for that great task. He speaks for God to us in sermon and sacraments. And when an individual voice is needed, he speaks for us to God in prayer.

Fourth, Reformed worship believes that the ordinary is much more important for our spiritual lives than the extraordinary. It is not the special meeting or the special music or the guest preacher that God is most likely to use to do his saving work. It is the ordinary worship and work of the church that, Sabbath by Sabbath, the Lord uses to build us up in the faith. The ordinary means of ministers, sermons, sacraments, songs, and prayers are where the critical action is for our spiritual well-being.

I was attracted by Reformed worship from the beginning of my Christian journey. After studying the Bible, theology, and history for many years, I am more convinced than ever that our Reformed approach to worship is not a matter of tradition or taste or style. Rather, it is a careful and faithful application of the teaching of the Bible. May we preserve and defend it zealously. Even more importantly, may we enter into it with hearts full of faith.

THIRTEEN

Passion

PSALM 66

This reflection on my spiritual journey started with a desire to show something of one person's attraction to Reformed Christianity. My experience is by no means unique, but it is perhaps unusual. Most Reformed Christians whom I know either were born into a Reformed church or became Reformed after being converted in some other branch of Christianity. I first learned about Christ and the Bible among the Reformed and have remained Reformed ever since.

My Calvinist convictions have not been preserved in a hot-house of isolation. I have had many experiences and encounters with non-Christian and non-Reformed points of view. My undergraduate and doctoral studies were in a decidedly secular university. I chose Gordon-Conwell Theological Seminary so that I could hear non-Reformed ideas fairly presented by non-Reformed teachers. I have worked closely with evangelicals and Pentecostals in the activities of the Theology Working Group of the Lausanne Committee for World Evangelization. I have had

141

a number of opportunities to lecture and discuss Lutheranism with staunch members of the Lutheran Church–Missouri Synod. Out of these experiences I have come to appreciate many aspects of the theology, piety, and service of evangelicals, Pentecostals, and Lutherans. My commitment to Reformed Christianity, however, has grown and deepened over the years. Confrontations and friendly discussions with those holding to other Christian traditions, as well as my own study, have convinced me more and more of the correctness of Calvinism.

Over the years I not only have studied the theology and history of Calvinism, but have also held Reformed teachings up against the standard of the Bible. The more carefully I have considered the Bible, the more I have been impressed with the faithfully biblical character of the Reformed faith. Such study of the Bible has always characterized Calvinists. Great Reformed theologians such as John Calvin, John Owen, Francis Turretin, and Charles Hodge were also great students of the Bible. Calvinism is not a "rational" system, seeking a rationalization from a few biblical texts. It is a theology that seeks simply and faithfully to summarize the teachings of Holy Scripture.

As I have grown in a knowledge of Calvinism, I have also grown in a passionate commitment to it. True Calvinism is always a religion of the heart more than a religion of the head. I fear that today in some Reformed circles, the head may have triumphed over the heart. Sometimes the legitimate satisfaction that we Reformed take in the profound scholarship of our heritage becomes an ugly arrogance. At other times we seem to focus excessively on a particular doctrine or set of ideas that produces a very unbalanced form of Calvinism.

What we need today is Calvinists who are committed to the full Calvinism of our great confessional standards. We cannot really claim to be Reformed if we do not share the

Reformed faith as summarized in our confessions. We are not true Calvinists if we have a peculiar and unconfessional view of the law, the covenant, faith, preaching, or worship. Rather, it is the fullness and balance of the confessions that express the true character of Calvinism.

Sometimes Reformed Christians are tempted to turn their churches into theological debating societies. Such churches, however, are not genuinely Reformed. True Reformed churches are for all who believe in Christ and love his Word. They are for the learned and the ignorant, for the reflective and the activist, for the rich and the poor. The great Reformed churches of Scotland, the Netherlands, and Hungary, for example, included every sort of person in society. That diversity should be true of our churches today. We should resist the American tendency for denominations to have a specific ethnic or socioeconomic character. American Reformed and Presbyterian churches too often have seemed to welcome only better-educated and more thoughtful Christians. We must labor to make our churches places of fellowship and welcome for all believers.

At the beginning of my spiritual journey, I found in song a way to express the passion of my commitment to Christ and his Word. Song is an avenue for all Christians to express their faith. It is a wonderful form of fellowship and clear demonstration of our unity. It is also a way for Christians to give voice to the feelings of their hearts.

In recent years, my passion for God's truth has been strengthened by my growing interest in and appreciation for the psalms. Historically the psalms were a key part of Reformed worship and piety. Almost all Reformed churches for two centuries sang psalms all or almost all the time. In the eighteenth century, some Reformed churches began to introduce hymns into their worship. That trend accelerated in the nineteenth century, especially in American Reformed and Presbyterian churches. Still, many conservative Scottish and Dutch churches continued to use psalms exclusively or at least extensively throughout the twentieth century.

One obvious effect of psalm-singing was that Reformed worshipers had the psalms well planted in their minds and hearts. If we should hide God's Word in our hearts that we might not sin against him (Ps. 119:11), singing the Word is one of the best ways to do that. Early Reformed leaders did not so much argue that we may sing only psalms as they argued that the psalms are the best songs to sing because they are divinely inspired.

The principal argument used to promote hymn-singing from the eighteenth century on has been that hymns are more clearly centered on Christ than are the psalms. This argument was known before the eighteenth century, but was not very persuasive among early Reformed people. Calvin and Luther believed that the psalms were filled with Christ. They also believed that if our prayers and sermons and sacraments are filled with Christ, then we will see Christ in the Psalter. But as the Lord's Supper became infrequent and sermons were too often moralistic, a great push developed to use hymns that preached the gospel. This impulse was strengthened by the increasingly revivalistic spirit of much American religion since the eighteenth century.

When I first started attending the Christian Reformed Church in 1961, most churches in that denomination sang about three psalms and one hymn in each service. Hymns had been approved for public worship only in 1934. But in most of those churches in the last forty years, the number of psalms used per service has declined dramatically. A similar decline has occurred in passion for Reformed doctrine and church life. Are the two related? It is difficult to be sure. What is sure is that Reformed Christianity can flourish only if its adherents have a passion for that faith. Certainly the psalms contribute significantly to building and expressing that passion.

Psalm 66 illustrates many of the reasons that I and so many other Reformed believers have loved the psalms. It is particularly appropriate for the purposes of this book when the psalmist declares, "Come and listen, all you who fear God; let me tell you what he has done for me" (v. 16). Each Christian experiences the goodness and grace of God personally. Each of us should be eager to declare the blessings of the Lord. In this book I have tried to testify to what the Lord has done for me.

In Psalm 66 the particular blessing celebrated by the psalmist is that God has heard and answered his prayer. Passionate faith leads to fervent prayer. The psalms show and express that truth over and over again. The Psalter is full of wonderful promises about prayer that encourage us to pray. This psalm shows that God hears the prayers of his own: "God has surely listened and heard my voice in prayer" (Ps. 66:19). But the psalm also reminds us that God does not automatically hear all prayers: "If I had cherished sin in my heart, the Lord would not have listened" (v. 18). The psalmist is not claiming sinless perfection as a prerequisite for prayer. He has already made it clear that he is a sinner when he spoke of bringing a burnt offering for sin. What is required is faith and love for the Lord and a repentant spirit in regard to sin. Each of us who seeks the Lord in faith recognizing our sin and seeking forgiveness can be assured that the Lord will hear us. As we read in Psalm 9:10, "Those who know your name will trust in you, for you, LORD, have never forsaken those who seek you."

This very personal element of the psalm follows after sections that reflect the universal and communal service of God.

Psalms often combine elements that seem strange and surprising. Yet the variety of elements that we find in the psalms assures us that our songs will have a truly inspired balance. The psalms balance the communal and the personal, as well as the objective and the subjective. They balance head and heart, intellect and emotion. They are the perfection of praise.

Many aspects of Reformed Christianity come to expression in Psalm 66. For example, the first four verses celebrate the sovereignty of God over all the earth. All the earth is urged to praise the Lord and recognize the awesomeness of his works. Here we see how God is supreme over all. He is Creator of all things, and he governs the course of all human history. God is indeed a personal God, close to each one of his people. But he is also sovereign over everything. He knows everything and maintains everything. With joy we must acknowledge that he is supreme even over his enemies. His universal power should lead us to confidence in his care for us.

As Calvinists, we find the sovereignty of our God empowering and energizing. All reality is his, and so we may participate in service and study in relation to any aspect of God's creation. We do not seek isolation or shelter from the life of this world; rather, we seek to honor God by showing his purpose for and claim over all spheres of life.

Psalm 66 also celebrates God's work of salvation, particularly in verses 5 to 7. These verses look back to the way in which God delivered his people from Egypt, the house of bondage. Despite the power of the oppressor, God rescued his people: "He turned the sea into dry land, they passed through the river on foot" (v. 6). God led them from slavery to the land of promise. He was their Savior.

Entering the promised land did not ensure that God's people would never have problems. The promised land was only a pointer forward to Christ and to the new heaven and the new earth. The Lord tested his people (Ps. 66:10) and laid burdens upon them (v. 11). But he also preserved them from falling utterly (v. 9) and brought them "to a place of abundance" (v. 12).

Who preserved and blessed the people of God? Who delivered them from their slavery to sin? To whom did the sacrifice for sin in the temple point? The answer is clear. Jesus Christ is the one who is the Savior and Shepherd of his own. Jesus fulfilled all the plans of his Father. He died effectively to save his people. He sent his Spirit to connect his people to himself and the saving benefits of his work. He is as sovereign in salvation as he is in all his other works.

The psalm calls us as the people of God to praise God. The command to praise begins and ends this psalm. Praise is the duty of the creation (v. 3) and the response to God's faithful care (Ps. 66:8). The praise of Israel expressed in Psalm 66 is our praise. We as Christians are as truly and fully the Israel of God as those believers who sang this psalm centuries ago. Truly the psalms unify the people of God in their praise. They bridge the differences between the Old Testament and the New, between different centuries, countries, and denominations. All God's people can take these songs upon their lips to express their faith and to sound their praise.

This praise, Psalm 66 reminds us, is supported by what we have come to see (Ps. 66:5) and to hear (v. 16) of the great works of God. We see in the Bible and in our own experience the love of God and of his people. When I was in high school, loving Christians called me to come and see the Savior whom they knew. My faith and Christian life have been sustained and nurtured through the years by the ministry of the congregations of which I have been part: the Alameda Christian Reformed Church, the Menlo Park Presbyterian Church, the

Orthodox Presbyterian Church of South Hamilton, Massachusetts, the Trinity Christian Reformed Church of Broomall, Pennsylvania, and the Escondido United Reformed Church.

On my first visit to a Reformed church many years ago, I was very impressed with the vigor of the singing. Today I am impressed with the vigor and content of the singing. The Psalter especially gives voice to my passionate commitment to the God revealed in Scripture. This God sometimes surprises me with the songs he has given me to sing. Sometimes the psalms contain difficult ideas, but even then they cause me to ponder the ways of God and to reform my thinking. Calvin was certainly right when he said that the Psalter expressed all the emotions of the Christian soul. As one scholar put it, the metrical psalms give Calvin's piety poetic power.

Over the years, the psalms have given voice to faith at some very important occasions in my life. At the baptisms of all three of my children, we sang Psalm 78:1–7. That psalm expressed the hope of my wife and me for our children:

> We will tell the next generation the praiseworthy deeds of the LORD, his power, and the wonders he has done. He decreed statutes for Jacob, and established the law in Israel, which he commanded our forefathers to teach their children, so the next generation would know them, even the children yet to be born, and they in turn would tell their children. Then they would put their trust in God and would not forget his deeds but would keep his commands. (Ps. 78:4b–7)

At my inauguration as president of Westminster Seminary California in 1993, we sang Psalm 68:1–6 to express our confidence in the power and love of the Lord:

May God arise, may his enemies be scattered; may his foes flee before him. . . . But may the righteous be glad and rejoice before God; may they be happy and joyful. . . . A father to the fatherless, a defender of widows, is God in his holy dwelling. (Ps. 68:1, 3, 5)

On our thirtieth wedding anniversary, I was speaking at a banquet of the synod of the Reformed Presbyterian Church. When the master of ceremonies learned that it was our anniversary, he led several hundred people in a beautiful a cappella rendition of Psalm 128 for us:

Blessed are all who fear the LORD, who walk in his ways. You will eat the fruit of your labor; blessings and prosperity will be yours. Your wife will be like a fruitful vine within your house; your sons will be like olive shoots around your table. Thus is the man blessed who fears the LORD. (Ps. 128:1–4)

In recent years at the funerals of friends, I have turned again and again to Psalm 103:7–18:

As a father has compassion on his children, so the LORD has compassion on those who fear him; for he knows how we are formed, he remembers that we are dust. As for man, his days are like grass, he flourishes like a flower of the field; the wind blows over it and it is gone, and its place remembers it no more. But from everlasting to everlasting the LORD's love is with those who fear him, and his righteousness with their children's children. . . . (Ps. 103:13–17)

At his request, I read Psalm 91 to my father-in-law, Charles Nemeth, on his deathbed. It was a psalm that had sustained him at many points in his life, especially when he was a prisoner of war in Germany for eighteen months during World War II:

> He who dwells in the shelter of the Most High will rest in the shadow of the Almighty. I will say of the LORD, "He is my refuge and my fortress, my God, in whom I trust." Surely he will save you from the fowler's snare and from the deadly pestilence. He will cover you with his feathers, and under his wings you will find refuge; his faithfulness will be your shield and rampart. . . . A thousand may fall at your side, ten thousand at your right hand, but it will not come near you. . . . "Because he loves me," says the LORD, "I will rescue him; I will protect him, for he acknowledges my name. He will call upon me, and I will answer him; I will be with him in trouble, I will deliver him and honor him. With long life will I satisfy him and show him my salvation."

The psalms have helped me to express my passion and zeal for Christ, his Word, and the Reformed faith. They have focused and united for me the theology, the worship, the piety, and the church life taught in the Scriptures. They have united for me head, heart, and mouth in the praise of the Lord. They are the soul of the Reformed faith. For forty years that faith has been for me a satisfying truth. As so many people have encouraged and helped me in living that faith, so I hope this book will help others to find the joys of Reformed Christianity.